U.S. Department of Justice
Office of Justice Programs
810 Seventh Street NW.
Washington, DC 20531

John Ashcroft
Attorney General

**Office of Justice Programs
World Wide Web Home Page**
www.ojp.usdoj.gov

**Bureau of Justice Assistance
World Wide Web Home Page**
www.ojp.usdoj.gov/BJA

For grant and funding information contact
U.S. Department of Justice Response Center
1–800–421–6770

This document was prepared by the International Centre for the Prevention of Crime under grant number 95-DD-BX-K001, awarded by the Bureau of Justice Assistance, Office of Justice Programs, U.S. Department of Justice. The opinions, findings, and conclusions or recommendations expressed in this document are those of the authors and do not necessarily represent the official position or policies of the U.S. Department of Justice.

> The Bureau of Justice Assistance is a component of the Office of Justice Programs, which also includes the Bureau of Justice Statistics, the National Institute of Justice, the Office of Juvenile Justice and Delinquency Prevention, and the Office for Victims of Crime.

THE ROLE OF LOCAL GOVERNMENT IN COMMUNITY SAFETY

April 2001

NCJ 184218

Prepared by the International Centre
for the Prevention of Crime

Foreword

Increasing numbers of people no longer view the safety of their neighborhoods as the sole responsibility of the police. Throughout the world, citizens in areas plagued by crime and violence are uniting to work with local government. Together, they have the knowledge and resources to identify and remove the sources of crime, drug use, and juvenile delinquency in their communities.

Developing and sustaining these partnerships requires strong local leadership from mayors, city managers, city planners, and other elected local officials. This monograph was prepared to help create that leadership by chronicling how local public officials have used community safety partnerships to build healthier communities.

A framework for using community-local government partnerships to reduce crime now exists based on the experiences of public officials in North America, Europe, Africa, and Australasia. This framework includes the following:

- Recognizing crime and safety as a quality-of-life issue.

- Working across jurisdictional boundaries.

- Recognizing the crucial role of political leadership.

- Developing tools and measures of success that involve the community and victims of crime.

The programs examined in this monograph illustrate that this framework works best when adapted to the specific needs of a community. Good governance requires that mayors and other key local officials develop the capacity to respond to those needs.

Bureau of Justice Assistance

Acknowledgments

This monograph was prepared for the Bureau of Justice Assistance, U.S. Department of Justice, by Margaret Shaw, who was assisted by Kathie Oginsky. Advice and knowledge were provided by Bernard Arsenault, Frantz Denat, Lily-Ann Gauthier, Daniel Sansfaçon, Claude Vezina, and Irvin Waller at the International Centre for the Prevention of Crime. The authors would like to thank the project advisory group for their insight, particularly Ed Summers of the U.S. Conference of Mayors, Robbie Callaway of the Boys & Girls Clubs of America, Linda Bowen of the National Funding Collaborative on Violence Prevention, Roberta Lesh of the International City/County Management Association, members of the National League of Cities, Michel Marcus of the European Forum for Urban Safety, and Sohail Husain of Crime Concern. The advice and help of staff from the National Crime Prevention Council, especially Theresa Kelly, Jack Calhoun, and Jim Copple, are gratefully acknowledged, as is the support of Jay Marshall and Patrick Coleman at the Bureau of Justice Assistance.

Contents

Executive Summary................................... ix

I. Community Safety in Cities, Suburbs, and Rural Areas 1
    Introduction...................................... 1
    Audience for This Monograph........................ 2
    Challenges for Local Governments 3
    Increasing Knowledge About Prevention 7
    Good Governance 10

II. The Emergence of Community Safety 11
    How Local Authorities in Other Countries Are Tackling
    Problems....................................... 11
    Focus on the City................................. 11
    Developing and Transitional Countries 12
    Recent European Initiatives 12
    Australasia and Canada 15
    Recent Developments in the United States 15
    Summary 18

III. A Framework for Community Safety 21
    A Strategy for Analyzing Problems and Mobilizing Resources .. 21
    Safe and Healthy Communities....................... 21
    Horizontal and Vertical Thinking 22
    Political Leadership 22
    Adapting Strategies to Local Needs.................... 22
    Building Capacity................................. 24
    Tools and Measurements of Success 25
    Basic Elements of the Local Government Approach......... 27

IV. Limitations, Lessons, and Conclusions. 29
   Partnership Problems and Information Sharing. 30
   Evaluation and Funding Issues 31
   Emerging Issues 32
   Centralized States and Federal Nations 32
   Summary 33

V. Examples From Practice. 35
   Borough of Brent, London, England: Community Safety and . . . .
   Community Empowerment. 35
   Toronto, Ontario, Canada: A Community Safety Strategy for
   the City. 37
   Brisbane, Queensland, Australia: Youth and Public Space
   Major Centers Project. 38
   Leichhardt Municipal Council, New South Wales, Australia:
   Draft Youth Social Plan. 40
   Freeport, Illinois: Coalition for a Safe Community 40
   Hartford, Connecticut: Neighborhood Problem-Solving
   Committees and the Comprehensive Communities Program. . . 41
   Salt Lake City, Utah: Changing the Way Government Works
   and the Comprehensive Communities Program 42
   Maryland HotSpot Communities: Reclaiming Our
   Neighborhoods 43
   METRAC, Toronto, Ontario, Canada: Taking Action
   Against Abuse of Women 43
   Amsterdam, The Hague, Rotterdam, and Utrecht,
   Netherlands: Big Cities Policy. 44
   EURO 2000 Football Cities Against Racism. 44
   Aix en Provence, France: Local Security Contract and
   Observatory 45

VI. Notes. 47

VII. References. 51

VIII. Resources and Addresses 55

IX. For More Information 59

Executive Summary

Good Governance

In recent years, mayors and municipal leaders throughout the United States have confronted increasing problems of community safety. These problems have affected not only urban centers but also small towns and rural municipalities. Many other countries have experienced similar rapid increases in crime that have only begun to decline in the past few years. The response of many governments has been to toughen their legal and justice systems, increasing policing capacities and penalties. Despite these efforts, the social and economic consequences of crime have been enormous:

- Expenditures on law enforcement have increased tremendously.

- Criminal sentences have become tougher.

- The number of offenders prosecuted and incarcerated has risen dramatically.

- Private security personnel have outstripped official law enforcement.

- Communities increasingly have resorted to fortifying neighborhoods.

- Crime has reduced the tax base of cities by driving out residents and businesses.

Traditionally, the public has viewed crime reduction as the responsibility of the police and the courts. However, in spite of increased expenditures, these institutions have been unable to contain the epidemic of crime. The result has been a loss of confidence in criminal justice systems and high levels of public concern about crime. Migration, rapid changes in populations, rising poverty levels, and income disparities continue to affect many countries. Crime prevention, rather than reaction or repression, has generally played a very minor role in addressing crime problems. To have an impact on current crime problems and avoid even greater problems in the future, a more balanced approach and perceptual shift by society are necessary.

This monograph was prepared for mayors, city managers, planners, and elected officials. It brings together information from around the United States and around the world on ways that public officials have used their authority to foster safer, healthier communities. More specifically, it outlines the following:

- Why change is necessary.

- Why communities can no longer leave safety to only the criminal justice system.

- How knowledge about the factors that lead to crime and insecurity has increased.

- How knowledge about how citizens can intervene effectively has increased.

- The leadership, strategies, and tools needed to bring about change.

- Examples of city-led projects.

- Lessons learned from past practice.

From Crime Prevention to Community Safety

Mayors and local government officials have played a major role in the evolution of community safety over the past 20 years in Europe, North America, Africa, and Australasia. Increasing numbers of initiatives target crime, victimization, and the social exclusion of individuals, minority groups, and neighborhoods. The links between poverty and social disadvantage and crime and victimization have shown that many agencies need to work together to prevent crime.

Mayors and local officials have come to see community safety as a basic human right and an important aspect of the quality of life in their communities. They have mobilized local partnerships with key actors—the police, government agencies, community organizations, and residents—to develop safe, secure, and vibrant communities in metropolitan as well as rural areas. These partnerships have made significant gains in how crime prevention is viewed. For example:

- The narrow focus on crime prevention has shifted to the broader issue of community safety and security as a public good.

- A consensus has developed about the need to work for community safety by tackling the social and economic conditions that foster crime and victimization.

- The common public view that community safety is the sole responsibility of the police has changed and people now recognize that governments, communities, and partnerships at all levels must be actively engaged.

- A recognition has evolved that local municipal leaders play a crucial role in protecting communities by organizing and motivating coalitions of local partners.

- Increasing evidence shows that intervention targeting risk factors can be effective and efficient in reducing crime and other social problems.

Executive Summary

A Framework for Community Safety

A framework for tackling community safety has emerged in recent years that can be used by local governments. This framework includes the following:

- Recognizing crime and safety as quality-of-life issues.

- Working across jurisdictional boundaries both horizontally and vertically.

- Recognizing the crucial role of political leadership.

- Adapting strategies to local needs on the basis of good analysis and targeted plans.

- Building capacity.

- Developing tools and measurements of success.

Limitations, Lessons Learned, and Examples From Practice

Defining communities and developing and sustaining partnerships are not simple tasks. Much can be learned from past successes and failures. Including community partnerships, understanding the links to underlying problems, looking at the strengths and assets of communities and individuals as well as risk factors, working on the analysis and planning process rather than focusing solely on programs that provide quick results, and addressing funding and evaluation are important activities that must be thought through.

Examples from Australasia, Europe, and North America, described in greater detail in chapter 5 of this monograph, illustrate how this framework has been adapted to the specific needs of individual communities. The initiatives are at different stages of development, and not all have reached the evaluation stage. They include 3-year strategic plans in large cities, projects targeting youth needs in public spaces, small town coalitions, neighborhood problem-solving committees, comprehensive community programs, hotspot initiatives that pool funding resources, coalitions targeting violence against women, groups of cities working on common problems or against racism, and local security contracts to help communities assess problems and create targeted action plans.

Mayors are strategically placed to make a difference in these endeavors. They can provide leadership to identify and mobilize key partners; authorize development of a rigorous safety audit that includes an action plan with short- and long-term goals; assign staff to implement, monitor, and evaluate the plan; and act as a conduit for exchanging expertise and good practices.

I. Community Safety in Cities, Suburbs, and Rural Areas

Introduction

Over the past 30 years, mayors and municipal leaders throughout the United States have faced increasing problems in keeping their communities safe. Disorder, crime, drugs, and guns have become daily reminders of the threats to living in safety and security. In the 1990s, these problems soared to their highest levels and had a major impact on children and adolescents. Young people increasingly have become the victims of violence, including homicides, and their involvement in serious crime and violence has also risen.

Tragedies such as the shootings at Columbine High School in Colorado have demonstrated that crime, insecurity, and violence are not limited to inner cities and large urban areas. Recent surveys of young people have found higher levels of drug use in suburban and rural areas than in cities. Guns, which are kept in millions of homes across America, have been a major factor in the increase in deaths of young people in the 1990s.

Increases in crime and violence have affected countries worldwide. The response of most governments was to toughen their legal and justice systems, increasing law enforcement expenditures and toughening penalties. The number of offenders prosecuted and incarcerated rose dramatically, and the number of private security personnel outstripped official law enforcement. The costs of maintaining criminal justice and correctional systems soared to unprecedented levels. Throughout this period, crime prevention, rather than repression, played a minor role. Furthermore, crime prevention was seen as largely the responsibility of the police. As this monograph makes clear, investing in the broader approach of community safety offers much greater rewards.

> BETWEEN 1980 AND 1997, NEARLY 38,000 JUVENILES WERE MURDERED IN THE UNITED STATES. THE RISE IN MURDERS OF JUVENILES BETWEEN 1984 AND 1993 WAS ALL FIREARM RELATED, AS WAS THE SUBSEQUENT DECLINE.
>
> —*Juvenile Offenders and Victims: 1999 National Report*

In the past few years, levels of recorded crime and violence have fallen significantly in a number of European countries and in North

America.[1] In the United States, the Federal Bureau of Investigation (FBI) reported a 7-percent drop in serious crime in 1999, the eighth consecutive year that the number of reported serious crimes fell. Reductions occurred in all types of crime, both violent and nonviolent, and they were found in all regions of the country. In Canada, crime rates have fallen for the past 8 years to the lowest crime level in 2 decades. In England and Wales, recorded crime fell 8 percent between 1993 and 1995, and a further 10 percent between 1995 and 1997, although violent crime rates are still rising.

> IN 1994, A UNITED NATIONS SURVEY OF 135 MAYORS FROM EVERY CONTINENT FOUND THAT CRIME AND VIOLENCE WAS THE FOURTH MOST SEVERE PROBLEM FACING THE WORLD'S CITIES.
>
> —International Colloquium of Mayors on Social Development, United Nations Development Program, 1994

Despite these decreases in crime rates, levels of crime and victimization are still well above those found in most countries 30 years ago and continue to be a great public concern. The public is often misinformed about criminal justice, as well as unaware of recent declines in crime and violence.[2] A number of trends suggest that unless city officials begin to approach crime problems differently, the growth, health, and well-being of cities will deteriorate.

There have been marked changes in the ways both local and national governments understand and tackle the problems of crime, violence, and insecurity. Many countries now see these problems as intricately linked to the health of neighborhoods and communities, to their quality of life, and as part of a wider concern about community safety and security.

This awareness has led to a focus on tackling the underlying problems of communities, based on careful analysis and planning in collaboration with citizens and local agencies. It represents a more concerted and multifaceted approach to prevention, and one that is likely to be more cost effective and bring wider benefits to the community than reacting after crime and tragedies have taken place.

Audience for This Monograph

This monograph is intended for use by mayors, city managers, planners, elected officials, and others who face the challenges of crime in their communities. These leaders are in a unique position to mobilize local agencies in the development of safe, secure, and vibrant communities. They are strategically placed to bring together the key actors in community crime prevention. Traditionally, they have been responsible for urban or rural planning and for developing ties with hospitals, schools, transportation companies, youth and social services, police, the judiciary, and the business community.

Community Safety in Cities, Suburbs, and Rural Areas

> OUR CITIES MUST BE PLACES WHERE HUMAN BEINGS LEAD FULFILLING LIVES IN DIGNITY, SAFETY, HAPPINESS, AND HOPE.
>
> —Habitat II Declaration, 1996

This monograph sets out the elements needed to bring about change. It presents information from around the world, including the United States, on how people in such positions have used their authority and energy to work toward safer communities. In the four chapters to follow, the monograph discusses

- Why change is necessary.

- Why the problems of crime can no longer be left solely to the justice system.

- How knowledge of the factors that lead to crime and violence has increased.

- How knowledge of ways to intervene effectively has increased.

- Strategies and tools needed to bring about change.

- Examples of local government and city-led projects that illustrate these themes.

Challenges for Local Governments

Growing Urbanization, Increasing Poverty, and Income Disparity

The 21st century presents huge challenges for mayors and local governments. Populations are expanding and migrating; towns and cities and their surrounding rural areas are growing rapidly; and levels of poverty and disparities between rich and poor are increasing. These developments have already had a significant impact on safety and security in many countries and their effects are likely to continue.

- Currently, between 40 percent and 55 percent of the world's population lives in urban centers. This proportion is expected to climb to 70 percent by 2020.

- Levels of poverty have risen in many Western countries despite increasing overall wealth.

- Throughout the world, income disparities between rich and poor families have increased.

- In developing countries, the poor tend to be concentrated in particular areas. In developed countries, conditions in many urban cores have declined while poverty rates in rural areas have increased.

- More women are living in poverty in both developed and developing countries. The number of single mothers has increased and they are likely to face more discrimination in job markets and housing than men.

- Due in part to systemic racism and discrimination, minority and immigrant populations are more likely to be living in poverty than the majority population.

Migration, immigration, and rapid growth are bringing about major changes to the ethnic character of urban populations. There are increases in indigenous populations moving to cities in Australia, New Zealand, North America, and South America. Western European countries have received increasing numbers of immigrants from Eastern European, Mediterranean, and North African countries.

Social Exclusion

In many countries, the concentration of poverty and social and economic problems in particular areas has led to talk about social exclusion. In Britain, France, and Germany, for example, increasing income disparity and concentration of poverty have been restricted to certain areas of the country.[3] Families who live in these areas are often the poorest in the country and include many immigrants and minorities. They often live in public housing estates in suburban or urban areas in the worst housing and environmental conditions.

People in such areas are excluded from taking part in the employment, health, safety, and prosperity enjoyed by the rest of the population. For these residents, poor health, crime, vandalism, drugs, unsupervised young people, litter, pollution, and lack of services add to the lack of safety and security in their lives.

> THE ISSUES FACING DEPRIVED NEIGHBOURHOODS ARE WELL KNOWN, AND MAKE SOBER READING. VIRTUALLY EVERY SOCIAL PROBLEM—CRIME, JOBLESSNESS, POOR HEALTH, UNDERACHIEVEMENT—IS SUBSTANTIALLY WORSE IN DEPRIVED AREAS. THERE IS GROWING EVIDENCE THAT THESE PROBLEMS REINFORCE ONE ANOTHER TO CREATE A DOWNWARD SPIRAL OF DEPRIVATION AND DECLINE.
>
> —*National Strategy for Neighbourhood Renewal: Neighbourhood Management*

In the United States, black communities are concentrated in inner cities. These areas experienced huge increases in youth crime, especially violence and youth homicide, in the early 1990s. In some areas, generations of children are also growing up without fathers and the increased imprisonment of women has left many of their children without close parental care. As a result, the network of social controls normally exercised by these people as parents, employees, friends, and neighbors has been reduced. This has major consequences for the future. The proportion of African-American, Asian/Pacific, Hispanic, and Native American children is expected to increase for the next 20 years.[4]

> BETWEEN 1988 AND 1997, THE NUMBER OF JUVENILES LIVING IN POVERTY GREW 13 PERCENT. THE NUMBER OF BLACK JUVENILES IN POVERTY DECREASED 2 PERCENT, COMPARED WITH A 21-PERCENT INCREASE FOR WHITE JUVENILES AND A 32-PERCENT INCREASE AMONG ASIAN/PACIFIC ISLANDERS.
>
> —*Juvenile Offenders and Victims: 1999 National Report*

Poverty in America has also increased outside the big cities, affecting the majority white population in rural areas, especially in the South. Between 1988 and 1997, for example, white juveniles living in poverty increased by 21 percent.

In a number of countries, problems for small- and medium-size towns and rural areas are growing. In England and Wales, some of the highest increases in reported crime in the 1990s have been in rural areas (Hosain, 1995). In the United States, while overall levels of reported crime fell for the past 8 years, there have been increases in crime and victimization in some American towns and rural areas such as those close to the Mexican border.

Unemployment, Drugs, and Young People

While North America is currently experiencing a better economic climate, in other countries changing labor and trade markets, technological developments, and the loss of unskilled jobs have increased the extent and duration of unemployment. This situation has especially affected young people, increasing their vulnerability to drugs, gangs, illness, and crime. More adolescents and young adults are now out of school, job training, or work. For example,

- In several European countries, youth unemployment rose between 1991 and 1995 from 15 percent to 20 percent for young men, and from 19 percent to 23 percent for young women (Pfeiffer, 1998).

- In Australia, full-time employment among teenagers fell from 56 percent in 1966 to 17 percent in 1993 (National Crime Prevention, 1999).

- In the United States, unemployment is especially high among African-American and Hispanic youth who have few educational skills. In one city, 63 percent did not graduate from high school (Rosenbaum et al., 1998).

Drug and alcohol abuse has become more prevalent among young people. This has been the case in European countries over the past 10 years, especially in areas of high unemployment.[5]

> SMOKING, DRINKING, AND DRUG USE AMONG YOUNG TEENS IS HIGHER IN RURAL AMERICA THAN IN THE NATION'S LARGE URBAN CENTERS.... SINCE 1990, DRUG LAW VIOLATIONS HAVE INCREASED MORE IN SMALL COMMUNITIES THAN IN LARGE CITIES; DRUGS ARE AS AVAILABLE IN SMALL COMMUNITIES AS THEY ARE IN LARGE CITIES, AND ADULT DRUG USE IN SUCH COMMUNITIES IS EQUAL TO THAT IN LARGE METROPOLITAN CENTERS. AT THE SAME TIME, MID-SIZE CITIES AND RURAL AREAS ARE LESS EQUIPPED TO DEAL WITH THE CONSEQUENCES.
>
> —*No Place to Hide*

In the United States, a recent study by the National Center on Addiction and Substance Abuse commissioned by the U.S. Conference of Mayors found that drug use was higher among young teens in mid-size cities and rural areas than in large metropolitan centers. Eighth graders in rural areas were 83 percent more likely to use crack cocaine and 70 percent more likely to have been intoxicated than their peers in large cities.

Offending and Victimization

In most countries, similar patterns of crime and victimization can be found in areas with many social and economic problems. We know from surveys in a number of countries that a small number of serious or persistent offenders are responsible for the majority of crime, especially serious crime. In many countries surveyed, 6 to 7 percent of young males are responsible for 50 to 70 percent of all crimes and 60 to 85 percent of serious and violent crimes (Loeber and Farrington, 1998).

A large overlap exists between victimization and offending. Those who are victimized tend to come from the same backgrounds and areas as those charged with offending, and people are often revictimized. A 1992 British survey found that 4 percent of victims suffer 40 percent of the crimes. In the United States, 50 percent of violent crime takes place in about 3 percent of addresses.

Violence against women and children is widespread. In developing countries, it is estimated that between 33 and 50 percent of all women are victims of violence from male partners.[6] In the United States, the number of children who are abused or neglected almost doubled between 1986 and 1993. We know that violence in the family often leads to other problems, including crime and ill health, as children grow up.

A major problem for many countries is the overrepresentation of indigenous and racial and ethnic minority groups in criminal justice systems. The proportions of immigrant children and second-generation children in justice systems have increased significantly in a number of European countries.[7]

Increasing Knowledge About Prevention

Risk and Prevention—People in Trouble Have Multiple Problems

More about the actual benefits of tackling community safety is known today and underlines the importance of investing in prevention. Evidence is accumulating about the factors that put people and areas at risk of becoming involved in crime and victimization. It is remarkable how similar these factors are from one country to another (Farrington, 2000). They include poverty and poor environment, poor parenting practices, family conflict and violence, early signs of aggressive behavior, spending too much time with friends and without adult contacts, doing poorly at school or dropping out, failing to learn good work skills or have employment opportunities, living in areas that lack services and facilities, and having access to drugs. These factors place children at risk and affect their development from birth to adulthood.

Early Intervention Is Effective

Researchers have studied the effectiveness of interventions, particularly in deprived areas where families and children are most at risk (Sherman et al., 1997; International Centre for the Prevention of Crime, 1999a). Interventions include

Figure 1
Prevention Programs Targeting Risk Factors for Youth Ages 12–18 Showing Reductions in Delinquency

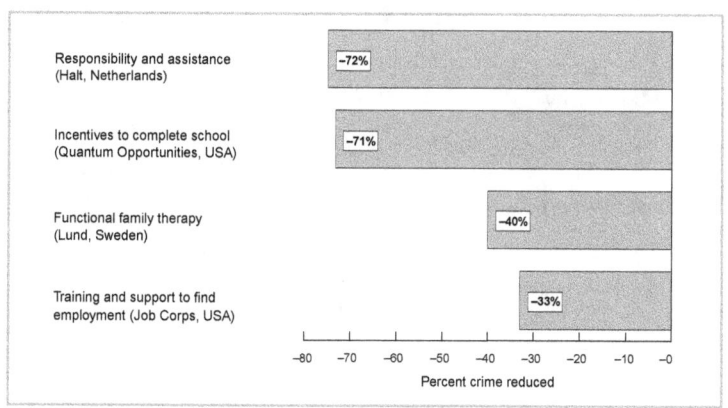

projects that provide preschool home visits and give children a head start in school. They have shown impressive long-term reductions in delinquency, lower school dropout rates, and improved quality of life for children and parents. Parent training and family therapy projects designed to strengthen parents' child-rearing capacities have similarly shown both short- and long-term benefits.

Other research has demonstrated that widespread intervention programs in schools can help reduce bullying behavior and improve school climate and academic performance, as well as decrease school disruptions and dropout rates. Programs targeting youth who have dropped out of school or been excluded have shown that work skills, job training, and mentoring can all help to reintegrate them into their communities.

Broken Windows and Brownfields

Many countries have demonstrated that changing the environment and situations that encourage crime are effective strategies. Cleaning up rundown streets, changing the design of buildings or public spaces, and improving lighting and surveillance all reduce the opportunities for crime. Studies of such efforts have demonstrated reductions in household burglary, car theft, graffiti, and vandalism. For example, in the Netherlands, England, and Wales, the rate of household

Figure 2
Reduction of Criminal Activity in Public Places Where Boys and Girls Clubs Are Present

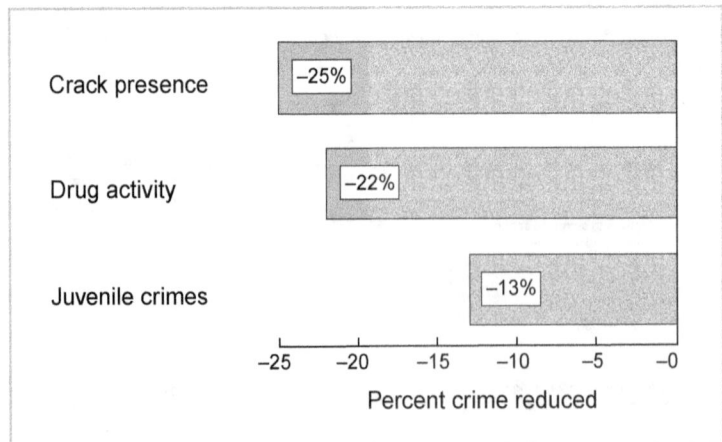

burglaries has been reduced by about 75 percent by neighborhood watch programs, improved security, and marking personal property. Vandalism and disorder have been reduced by increasing surveillance on public transportation, closed-circuit television cameras, and requiring bar owners to change their serving practices. Much of this work has been initiated by the police in collaboration with local mayors, agencies, and community members.

These experiences demonstrate that approaches that are carefully planned and build on past knowledge reduce crime and reduce risk factors. They improve the lives of those involved and demonstrate that the most effective intervention projects are those that include agencies and institutions at the local government level: community organizations, families, police departments, school systems, labor unions, social service agencies, youth groups, housing developments, and justice systems.

Costly Examples

Dealing with the impact of crime is expensive. Although people may feel that something is being done when tough measures are taken against crime, this approach does not deal with the long-term consequences for families or help to prevent future delinquency. Children growing up in poverty, lacking services and supports, are vulnerable to long-term involvement in drug use and crime. Most prisoners will eventually be released from prison, but generations of children may have been raised without close parental care.

Figure 3
Cost of Crime Per Capita in Selected Countries

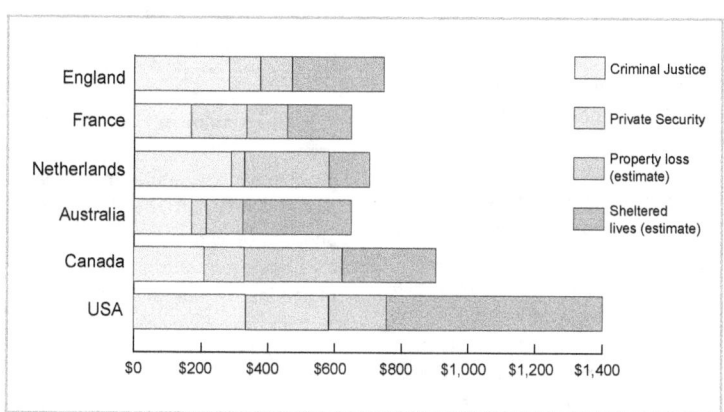

There are considerable differences in the costs and benefits of action to prevent crime, compared with action after it takes place. Preventive action can be up to 10 times more cost effective than traditional control measures such as incarceration. Money invested in crime prevention also brings benefits such as improved education, job skills, and health.

> LOCAL LEADERS ARE ACUTELY AWARE OF THE MANY COSTS OF CRIME TO THE COMMUNITY AND THE NEED TO REDUCE OR PREVENT IT. OUTLAYS FOR LOCAL LAW ENFORCEMENT AND OTHER CRIMINAL JUSTICE ELEMENTS SKYROCKET; LOCALLY SUPPORTED HOSPITALS, SOCIAL SERVICES, AND SCHOOLS SUFFER AS THEY ABSORB THE COSTS OF CRIME AND ITS EFFECTS ON VICTIMS.
>
> —*Creating a Blueprint for Community Safety*

Good Governance

The social and economic consequences of crime are enormous. Expenditures on policing, the courts, prisons, and private security have grown enormously. Crime causes serious problems for local government when towns or city centers decay as residents, businesses, and jobs move away, reducing the tax base. Traditionally, crime prevention has been regarded as the responsibility of police and prosecutors. Yet in spite of increased expenditures, they have not been able to contain the huge increases in crime that have occurred over the past 40 years.

Fear of crime and violence has led to fortifying neighborhoods, excluding individuals, and imposing tougher sentences. These reactions do not deal with the long-term problems of the excluded nor with the spread of crime and insecurity to small cities and rural areas in the United States. In many countries, the public has lost confidence in criminal justice systems. An approach is needed that balances good policing and justice with well-planned prevention.

Public opinion shows consistent support for prevention. A 1994 survey found that 61 percent of Canadians felt government resources should be spent on prevention rather than criminal justice. In America, 54 percent felt increased spending on social and economic problems, rather than police or prisons, was a more effective response to crime.

To have an impact on current crime problems and avoid greater problems in the future, municipal leaders must shift how they think and act. Seeing community safety as a basic human right, good governance insists that local government leaders bear the primary responsibility for fostering safe and healthy communities.

II. The Emergence of Community Safety

How Local Authorities in Other Countries Are Tackling Problems

In recent years, in an increasing number of countries, crime prevention projects have reduced the opportunities and increased the risks of committing crime by changing policing practices or the city environment. Some countries have focused on renewing poor neighborhoods and others on strengthening the ability of residents to integrate better into society. In both cases there has been an emergence of community-based strategies and expertise, bringing together local partnerships, with local authorities playing a key role. There has been a shift from the narrower notion of crime prevention as something the police do to the broader idea of community safety, which is a community responsibility.

Focus on the City

Since the 1980s city leaders have begun to take a leadership role in crime prevention. In France, for example, the Mayors Commission on Security (Bonnemaison, 1982) led to the creation, in 1982, of a system of city contracts with mayors that enabled them to create local crime prevention councils. Under the leadership of their mayors, these councils brought together a range of local people and agencies to develop prevention projects in their communities throughout France.[8] The European Forum for Urban Safety (EFUS) was set up in 1987 to link mayors across Europe, developing community safety through strong city partnerships. EFUS now includes more than 100 local authorities.

In the past two decades, a series of international meetings has brought together mayors, police executives, judges, community leaders, policymakers, crime prevention practitioners, and researchers to discuss ways of creating safer communities. Meetings were held in Strasbourg (1986), Barcelona (1987), Montreal (1989), Paris (1991), and Vancouver (1996). The U.S. Conference of Mayors and the National League of Cities took part in the first European and North American Conference on Urban Safety and Crime Prevention in Montreal in 1989. The Federation of Canadian Municipalities and EFUS were also represented, and the conference established an Agenda for Safer Cities. These organizations took part in a followup conference in Paris (1991) that brought together 1,600 people from 65 countries, who set out seven steps to make world communities safer.

Developing and Transitional Countries

Attempts to establish city-based crime prevention strategies have also been made in developing countries.[9] A Latin American forum on urban safety was held in Cordoba in 1998. In Africa, an International Forum of Mayors for Safer Cities was held in Johannesburg in 1998, bringing together nearly 60 mayors from across the continent (Institute for Security Studies, 1999). A Safer

> CITIES THAT ARE SAFE FOR ALL PEOPLE WILL, IN TURN, MAKE THE WHOLE WORLD A SAFER PLACE, FOR FEAR OF CRIME AND VIOLENCE IMPRISONS PEOPLE IN THEIR HOMES AND MAKES THE REALIZATION OF ALL OTHER HUMAN RIGHTS MORE DIFFICULT TO ACHIEVE.... PREVENTION STRATEGIES ADDRESSING THE ROOT CAUSES OF URBAN CRIME HOLD CONSIDERABLE PROMISE.
>
> —U.N. Secretary General Kofi Annan, 1998

Cities Program was also launched in 1996, with pilot projects in Johannesburg, Durban, Dar es Salaam, and Abidjan.[10] South Africa has placed a strong emphasis on community-based solutions and local autonomy. Its 1999 manual for local community-based crime prevention, *Making South Africa Safe*, provides a clear framework for developing and implementing local strategies.

> KINGSMEAD ESTATE, HACKNEY, UNITED KINGDOM
>
> STARTING WITH CIVIL INJUNCTIONS TO STOP GANGS AND CRIMINAL INTIMIDATION, THIS LOCAL COUNCIL, TENANTS, AND POLICE PARTNERSHIP HAS MOVED ON TO COMMUNITY DEVELOPMENT, E.G., RENOVATING PROPERTIES AND STARTING DROP-IN CENTERS AND ACTIVITIES FOR YOUNG PEOPLE.... BURGLARIES FELL FROM 340 IN 1992 TO 50 IN 1993 AND RESIDENTS HAVE GAINED CONFIDENCE.
>
> —*Reducing Neighbourhood Crime*

Recent European Initiatives

In more than 20 countries, local authorities and communities are developing community-based policies and programs with the support of national government bodies that promote community safety.

In England and Wales, local governments have been mobilized by two major initiatives that began in 1998. Under the Crime and Disorder Act, each local authority and its police force must establish a multiagency Community Safety Partnership to include health, probation, and other authorities, as well as youth representatives. In 3-year cycles, these partnerships will conduct local audits of crime, victimization, and disorder, set priorities for action, and develop and initiate strategic plans.[11]

Authorities recognize that crime prevention partnerships are likely to be more effective than single agencies (such as a police department or a school system) working alone, and that targeted strategies, using rigorous analysis, monitoring, and evaluation, produce results.

These community safety partnerships are part of the new National Strategy for Neighbourhood Renewal. Since 1998, the Social Exclusion Unit has produced a series of 18 Policy Action Team reports as part of this strategy. The reports outline ways to achieve four objectives: less long-term unemployment, less crime, better health, and better qualifications.[12]

Local governments can apply for some of the $415 million in funding for developing crime reduction strategies targeted to high-risk crime areas and families. In addition, 10 percent of this money is to be spent on evaluating these programs to assess short- and long-term benefits as well as their costs. A major emphasis has been placed on what is called "joined-up thinking," trying to work across agency boundaries at the local, regional, and national levels (Social Exclusion Unit, 2000b).

In France, local security contracts (or CLS) have been in existence for more than 15 years. They are based on the notion that security equals prevention plus sanction and reintegration. Prevention and reintegration are seen as the responsibility of everyone in the community. The contracts require local partnerships to foster access to justice and victim assistance, to create new youth jobs and training, and to take action to prevent delinquency through youth employment, parent support, and sports and cultural programs that meet local needs.

Many of the new jobs, such as social mediation agents and local security assistants, will be filled by youth from disadvantaged areas with high levels of unemployment.[13] The local security contracts are

HANKO, FINLAND

IN 1991, THIS SMALL CITY OF 11,000 CHANGED ITS CHILD WELFARE POLICIES AWAY FROM INSTITUTIONAL CARE; IMPLEMENTED A NIGHTLIFE STREET PATROL PROGRAM TO INCREASE INFORMAL SOCIAL CONTROL; AND DEVELOPED EMPLOYMENT AND APPRENTICESHIP PROGRAMS TO REDUCE TRUANCY, SUBSTANCE ABUSE, CRIME, AND ANTISOCIAL BEHAVIOR. THE RESULT WAS A 41-PERCENT REDUCTION IN PROPERTY CRIMES BY JUVENILES, AND A 50-PERCENT REDUCTION IN WELFARE COSTS BETWEEN 1991 AND 1993.

—*100 Crime Prevention Programs To Inspire Action Across the World* embedded within the larger city contracts concerned with overall social and economic renewal and development.

Local Security Contracts

In France, some 378 city contracts have been signed with mayors, and 720 local security contracts will be completed covering most large urban areas in the country. Job creation activities will include the appointment of 20,000 social-mediation agents to work on prevention and security issues at the local level, and 15,000 local security assistants attached to police departments.

Belgium has adopted the French system of funding city contracts. In the past 6 years, more than 30 municipal crime prevention councils, as well as the 5 major cities and the 7 districts of Brussels, have signed contracts. The councils are usually required to appoint a responsible officer to administer and develop their activities to meet local needs.

Netherlands developed the Major Cities Policy in 1996 to respond to the crisis in its cities. This policy focuses on the concentration of unemployment, family breakdown, decaying neighborhoods and public spaces, drug addiction, and crime. Agreements have been reached between local government leaders in the 4 major cities and 21 medium-size cities and with national government ministries. The agreements provide funds for the development of strategies and programs targeting those issues.

In 1999, the Integral Programme on Safety and Security was launched to target youth crime and safety, drug-related problems, street violence, robberies, vehicle-related crime, and traffic safety. The program emphasizes working jointly across ministries at the municipal level and with community and business groups. Current projects target at-risk children and youth, particularly ethnic minorities, by providing healthy start programs and projects that aim to reduce school dropout and unemployment rates.

The Stadswacht or City Guards program in Dordrecht, Holland, recruits and trains the long-term unemployed to work as uniformed civilian police. They provide information for the police and municipality on crime and disorder problems and solutions, as well as helping tourists. . . . There has been a 17-percent reduction in crime in the areas they patrol since they were introduced.

—*100 Crime Prevention Programs to Inspire Action Across the World*

Australasia and Canada

The region known as Australasia comprises New Zealand, Australia, Tasmania, and Melanesia. In New Zealand, 62 local authorities have signed contracts to set up Safer Community Councils modeled on the French contract system. Their goal is to enhance the ability of local communities to prevent crime and deal with local crime-related problems (Hamilton, 1999). In Australia, cities and shires across the provinces of Victoria, South Australia, and Queensland have developed safer city strategies and aids to local governments

In 1990, an escalating illicit drug trade and a high crime rate in the Little Burgundy area of Montreal led to the creation of a neighborhood coalition with municipal departments, residents, and the police. The coalition developed a new sports complex, better libraries, transportation, lighting, and security; encouraged job creation; and provided better social assistance services. They developed a community newspaper and an annual residents festival. There was a 46-percent reduction in crime after the first 3 years, and a reduction in the drug trade.

—*100 Crime Prevention Programs To Inspire Action Across the World*

and their partners since the mid-1990s (International Centre for the Prevention of Crime, 1999b; White, 1998).

In Canada, the Federation of Canadian Municipalities and local authorities in cities such as Montreal, Toronto, and Kitchener have worked together to create community safety plans. The federal government, through its National Crime Prevention Centre, has recently put $27 million (Canadian) into three major funding programs: a community mobilization program, a crime prevention investment fund, and a crime prevention partnership program. These programs stimulate locally based community crime prevention efforts that focus on social development and develop tools and knowledge about partnership development, needs assessment, plan development, best practices, effective intervention, and evaluation.

Recent Developments in the United States

In the United States, city mayors and local authorities have begun to play a more active role in community safety over the past decade. The increase and spread of crime, victimization, and violence in the late 1980s and early 1990s associated with the crack cocaine epidemic, youth violence and homicides, and rapidly increasing prison populations have all helped to spur a search for new approaches. Apart from their involvement at international conferences, the U.S. Conference of Mayors and the National League of Cities have undertaken surveys and developed working groups on aspects of crime prevention including issues such as drugs and youth.

MUSCLE and T-CAP: Combining Municipal and Grassroots Energies

In 1991, the severity of crime and its increase led the mayors of eight Texas cities to form Mayors United on Safety, Crime and Law Enforcement (MUSCLE).[14] Their cities were home to 35 percent of the population in Texas, but 60 percent of violent crimes across the state. They developed legislative proposals and a major crime prevention initiative. The Texas City Action Plan to Prevent Crime (T-CAP) included support from officials in seven of the cities (El Paso decided not to participate). The mayors felt that developing their programs simultaneously would enable them to benefit from each others' experiences.

T-CAP, according to the National Crime Prevention Council (NCPC), was able to

- Create a road map to reach goals.

- Focus effort where action was needed and productive.

- Avoid the "business as usual" trap.

- Maximize use of existing resources.

- Tailor its product to local needs.

- Build new commitments, partnerships, and resources.

- Reflect and incorporate changes in the real world outside the planning room.

- Deal more effectively with contingencies and emergencies.

The U.S. Government funded NCPC to act as a facilitator. This responsibility included hiring a state coordinator, developing a planning prototype, training staff, and developing local material and manuals to assist in the implementation of community-based plans. Each city established a coalition of municipal agencies and community leaders under the mayor's leadership; assessed the community's safety needs; created a task force of residents and experts to deal with specific issues; and developed a comprehensive implementation plan.

The plans were diverse, reflecting local interests and issues. They ranged from setting up a youth sports network and organizations to help poor neighborhoods to implementing school curriculum changes and crime prevention resource centers. The result was that "the role and value of crime prevention grew, along with people's capacity for action" (National Crime Prevention Council, 1994: 4). T-CAP demonstrated that cities have considerable knowledge. Municipal agencies such

The Emergence of Community Safety

as parks, sanitation, traffic, youth services, health, and education departments all provided information that provided a detailed picture of how problems of violence and crime are linked with other social issues and how intervention programs work. The costs of the program were relatively modest, with $450,000 in federal funding and $5,000 to $10,000 from participating cities, as well as in-kind support.

Comprehensive Community Programs

In the 1990s, several major federal funding initiatives facilitated local community-based crime prevention actions that responded to local needs. They recognized that fragmented services waste resources and that it is better to work collectively rather than in isolation. These initiatives include Operation Weed and Seed, Pulling America's Communities Together (PACT), and the Comprehensive Communities Program (CCP). They have three major differences from earlier funding approaches:

- They fund comprehensive rather than single-issue or service programs.

- They target key situational, social, and economic factors associated with crime using multidisciplinary approaches.

- They combine grassroots and local initiatives with funding and support from higher levels of government.

CCP was launched in 1994 by the Bureau of Justice Assistance (BJA) to integrate law enforcement with social programs. The program empowers local leaders to control the allocation of funds. Fifteen CCP sites have been funded.[15]

A Few Signs That CCP Is Working

In Baltimore, trash has been removed, crackhouses have been shut down, and properties have been put into receivership to be managed on behalf of neighborhoods. Associations have been formed to help renters buy homes that were formerly abandoned.

In Columbia, police can now park both their personal and police cars in public housing developments without fear of vandalism, and pizza is again being delivered to residents.

In Boston, the head of a local business association is asking merchants to remove the metal shields over their doorways and windows.

In Salt Lake City and Fort Worth, residents are asking for a say in local government and an opportunity to voice their opinions about local problems.

—*Comprehensive Communities Program: A Preliminary Report*

Communities were required to take the initiative to develop partnerships, to have an existing local coordinating structure, and to develop community policing. In many cases CCP communities have built on their earlier experiences of local coalitions developed under T–CAP or Weed and Seed funding. The expansion of community policing as a requirement has helped communities develop strategies. They have learned from their mistakes and successes. Self-evaluation and accountability have usually been built into the contracts.

Examples of the successes of some of these programs are highlighted in the report *Six Safer Cities*, which outlines their main strategies and programs (National Crime Prevention Council, 1999a). The six cities (Boston, Denver, Fort Worth, Hartford, New York City, and San Diego) have all achieved reductions in crime greater than the national average. The shrinking of the youth population responsible for much crime, changes in the drug market, improved economic stability, and increases in youth employment have contributed to the decline in recorded crime, along with the multiagency and local community-based initiatives. In Boston, New York City, and Fort Worth, the police took the lead in initiating the projects. In Denver, Hartford, and San Diego, it was the mayor and city council who assumed the leadership role. In all cases, city representatives worked with multi-agency and community coalitions to develop locally tailored programs.

Small Cities Initiative

Small towns and rural municipalities have also developed comprehensive programs. Approximately 70 percent of Americans live in towns and cities of between 25,000 and 50,000 people. The Small Cities Initiative was developed by NCPC in 1997 to provide assistance to seven cities through federal, state, and local funding.[16] There are now 10 cities and 1 county in the initiative, developing strategies that use their close networks and resources.

Summary

Looking at the involvement of local authorities across a number of countries in Europe, North America, Africa, and Australasia—in large metropolitan areas as well as small cities and rural areas—several important trends are apparent:

- A shift from a relatively narrow focus on crime prevention to the broader issue of community safety and security as a public good.

- A developing consensus about the need to work for community safety by tackling the social and economic conditions that foster crime and victimization.

- A shift in public view from seeing the primary responsibility for community safety as that of the police to recognizing that governments, communities, and partnerships at all levels need to be actively engaged in reducing crime.

- A recognition of the crucial role that local municipal leaders play in this process through organizing and motivating coalitions of local partners to create healthy and safe communities.

- An increase in evidence that intervention targeting risk factors can be effective in reducing crime and other social problems.

- A realization that intervention can be cost effective compared with criminal justice solutions.

What has emerged in recent years is a framework for understanding community safety and a strategy for creating it that can be used by local governments. This framework is outlined in the next chapter.

III. A Framework for Community Safety

A Strategy for Analyzing Problems and Mobilizing Resources

This chapter outlines major elements of a framework for fostering community safety that are being used by local governments in many countries. The approach includes the following:

- Recognizing community safety as a right and an issue of the quality of life in healthy communities.

- Working horizontally as well as vertically across jurisdictional boundaries.

- Understanding the crucial role of political leadership.

- Adapting strategies to local needs on the basis of good analysis and targeted plans.

- Building capacity.

- Developing tools and measurements of success.

Safe and Healthy Communities

Citizens are entitled to safe and healthy communities. Protecting communities from crime or reestablishing levels of safety can be tackled in the same way as public health issues. A preventive public health approach, such as that used to reduce the incidence of heart disease, involves looking for factors that increase the risks of development. Looking at patterns of economic and social problems in a neighborhood or community, as well as patterns of crime, disorder, and victimization, makes it easier to see how and where to intervene. In the United States, the Centers for Disease Control and Prevention has been active in demonstrating how crime and violence can be seen as health problems.

COMMUNITIES THAT CARE IN SEATTLE, WASHINGTON, USES A PUBLIC HEALTH APPROACH. ITS MAIN GOALS ARE TO REDUCE DELINQUENCY AND DRUG USE BY COMBINING KNOWLEDGE ABOUT RISK AND PROTECTIVE FACTORS AND EFFECTIVE INTERVENTIONS WITH CAREFULLY PLANNED COMMUNITY MOBILIZATION. A COMMUNITY BOARD OF KEY LOCAL LEADERS, RESIDENTS, AND AGENCIES UNDERTAKES AN ASSESSMENT OF THE MAIN RISK AND PROTECTIVE FACTORS AND DEVELOPS A STRATEGY FOR INTERVENTION.

—*Communities That Care Prevention Strategies*

Similar programs are now being developed in the United Kingdom (Nuttall et al., 1998), Scotland, Netherlands (Junger-Tas, 1997), and the United States.

This approach encourages broad responses to crime for victims. Recognition of the long-term impact of crime on victims' health has resulted in programs that provide ongoing community assistance beyond immediate victim support. An example is a partnership in Boston to help youth victims of crime prevent reinjury, given that the risk of revictimization is high once someone has been victimized. In London, the local health service is developing a health strategy that recognizes the links between crime, disorder, and victimization with health (Crime Concern, 1999).

Horizontal and Vertical Thinking

Working across jurisdictional and geographic boundaries is important to community crime prevention for two reasons. First, isolated projects are unlikely to be effective in dealing with the multiple problems facing families living in deprived and high-crime areas. In their review of what works in preventing crime, Sherman and colleagues (1997) concluded that effective crime prevention in high-violence neighborhoods requires simultaneous intervention by many local institutions.

Second, effective local government action requires all the municipal services to work together rather than in isolation. It requires support from higher levels of government and links among national, state, regional, or provincial authorities. This recognition has motivated policies in England, Wales, and France that stress the importance of working across jurisdictions and developing "joined-up thinking."

A 1996 study by the National League of Cities showed that local elected officials and administrators provide leadership in four ways:

- They model and set the tone for public discourse and problem solving.

- They use the power of their office to convey messages to their community.

- They help shape the processes and programs.

- They use team-building skills to build trust and communication and resolve conflicts.

Political Leadership

For community crime prevention to work, real commitment and leadership must come from someone at a high level who takes responsibility for putting the issues of community safety on the policy agenda.

Often the mayor, a chief executive of a local authority, or a police chief is the key person at the local government level. In some cases a specific body or community safety officer is appointed and given the

A Framework for Community Safety

The National Crime Prevention Council asked a range of local government-community coalitions what motivated them to work together. The answers varied considerably, depending on local circumstances and events:

- A pending crisis and a sense that the situation would worsen without immediate action.

- Community pressure arising from a catalyzing event or tragedy.

- Success of a single-issue initiative.

- Support from outside.

- Realization that single-focus interventions cannot deal with complex issues.

- Desire to sustain safe neighborhoods and avert a crisis.

responsibility for developing partnerships and plans. While local governments are best placed to give citizens a role in the development of their neighborhoods, their leaders can play a number of major roles:

- Preventive: educating the population and the media.

- Promotional: encouraging the development of community safety.

- Active: providing aid to victims and facilitating the mediation and resolution of local disputes and conflicts.

- Knowledge providers: developing and planning.

- Articulative: developing internal and external requirements and constraints.

- Constructive: putting in place a permanent local structure with local coordination and the necessary resources.

Adapting Strategies to Local Needs

Thorough and careful analysis of local problems is an important element in a community safety framework. Analysis includes studies on local factors that place people most at risk and effective intervention strategies for reducing those risks.

A careful analysis of local problems, sometimes called a safety audit or a security diagnosis, requires the collection of detailed information about crime, victimization, disorder, and fear of crime in a neighborhood or across a whole municipality. This information can include police statistics, census data, and the results of local surveys of residents, businesses, schools, transportation officials, and hospitals. But the analysis needs to go further by looking at the links to a range of other problems such as housing, jobs, unemployment, school dropout rates, youth facilities, and other existing community resources.

Neighborhood management projects are most likely to be successful if they include the following five elements:

* Someone with overall responsibility at the neighborhood level.

* Community involvement and leadership.

* The tools to get things done.

* A systematic, planned approach to tackling local problems.

* Effective delivery mechanisms.

—*National Strategy for Neighbourhood Renewal: Neighbourhood Management*

A good security diagnosis can take between 6 months and 1 year to complete. This careful analysis allows for the development of targeted strategies and plans. Once projects have begun, they need to be monitored and evaluated continuously to see if they are working as planned or need to be modified. The more focused the strategy, the more successful it is likely to be.

Building Capacity

Developing partnerships, getting funding or local security contracts, conducting a security diagnosis or safety audit, developing an action plan, and implementing, evaluating, and sustaining the plan are not simple tasks. They require expertise, information, and approaches that may be very different from traditional ways of working.

Building capacity includes the development of the skills, practical knowledge, experience, and tools required to undertake effective community-based action. Many countries recognize the importance of capacity building. A growing range of training programs for community safety personnel on monitoring and evaluating special issues such as drugs, domestic violence, and mental health and providing ongoing technical assistance, advice, and support is now being developed.

In European countries, training is provided by organizations such as the European Forum for Urban Safety, Crime Concern, the London Borough of Brent in England and Wales, and Copping On in Ireland. This includes training for specific interventions such as mentoring or working with at-risk youth, and providing governments and community safety partnerships with a range of skills. In England and Wales, local governments also have national guidelines on setting up partnerships, developing safety audits, and evaluating the outcome of programs.

In the United States, CCPs have been provided with technical assistance and budget and program guidelines by such federal funders as BJA. The National Funding Collaborative on Violence Prevention (NFCVP) and National Crime Prevention Council (NCPC) already provide training for collaborative and local authority community safety initiatives. NCPC is also developing a curriculum training program with the University of Kansas for use over the Web.

The Press and the Media

Building capacity to develop public awareness of community-based prevention and to utilize the media appropriately is another important area. This component includes showing the benefits and successes of well-planned strategies and informing the public of stories about how problems have been solved. Mayors, local agency staff, the police, community safety professionals, community members, researchers, and evaluators all need training and clear policies to develop their ability to communicate with the media. It is important to present initiatives as citizen projects to help to ensure community ownership.

Local Security Contracts and Funding

Community projects require funding for startup, pilot projects, and implementation, but they also need long-term funding. Resources are needed to sustain action at the local level, to demonstrate the effectiveness and efficiency of projects, and to disseminate information and best practices through transfer and training. One way to do this is through local security or community safety contracts that allow local partnerships to develop and tailor plans to their own needs. In many cases, projects must be monitored and evaluated.

A second way to fund initiatives is pooling existing funding from local government agencies such as schools, community organizations, private foundations and businesses. NFCVP pools resources from public and private sources to help local community coalitions develop programs to reduce violence.

Tools and Measurements of Success

Tools are needed to identify trends in crime such as where it occurs and associated social and economic problems. Tools are also needed to target risk factors underlying those problems and to evaluate the process and impact of programs.

Quality of Life and Social Safety: Ghent, Belgium

In 1997, a Safety Contract enabled a high-rise "problem estate" to improve its physical conditions and quality of life; reduce drug dealing, car theft, and burglaries; and escape from its problem image. More than 300 residents, local government, and the police developed and carried out the plan.

—European Crime Prevention Awards, 1999

A great deal of information on community-based strategy development is now accessible in many countries, including compendiums of best practice programs, guides and how-to manuals, summaries of evaluated research, and detailed blueprints for setting up tested, effective programs. Examples from the United States are provided in the following publications: *Innovative State and Local Programs* (BJA, 1997); *Creating a Blueprint for Community Safety* (NCPC, 1998); *Standing in the Gap* (NCPC, 1999b); *Blueprints for Violence Prevention* (CSPV, 1997); and *150 Tested Strategies To Prevent Crime From Small Cities, Counties, and Rural Communities* (NCPC, 2000).[17]

Working collectively at the neighborhood level requires good information. To succeed, community safety partnerships need to know the range of social, economic, health, and environmental problems apart from information on crime and disorder typically available from police records. One solution in Europe has been the creation of observatories, permanent centers that collate information on a range of social, economic, and health indicators, including criminal justice measures. Their effectiveness depends on the accuracy of the data they collect, the diversity of their sources, and the quality of their observations.

In Lille, France, the neighborhood of Eurolille set up an observatory in 1995 to collect information about the frequency and location of crime and mental health problems and about the capacity of neighborhoods to respond to these problems. It surveyed residents, disadvantaged groups, and young people to assess their views on problems and solutions. Built in 1990, Eurolille has large residential, shopping, entertainment, and commercial sectors and a rapid transport system. It established its observatory to collate information as a basis for developing a joint action plan and neighborhood safety policy. Businesses were required to contribute resources to the process. The purpose is to develop a healthy social climate in Eurolille, reduce crises, and encourage interaction between institutions, agencies, and individuals (European Forum for Urban Safety, 1996).

Another tool used effectively by communities is crime mapping, which involves systematically collecting data and assessing the location and development of specific problems in neighborhoods. Recent initiatives of this type in the United States include Strategic Approaches to Community Safety Initiatives and the Arrestee Drug Abuse Monitoring Program.

In addition, communities use benchmarking to compare practices and performances of different service providers, identify good practices, and foster collaboration between providers, or to establish a basis for subsequent evaluation of programs. By using standardized procedures and measures, comparisons can be made between programs.

Basic Elements of the Local Government Approach

The basic elements of the local government approach to community safety include the following:

- Identification and mobilization of key partners led by local city authorities and involvement of local agencies, community organizations, police and justice systems, and the private sector.

- A rigorous assessment or security diagnosis of local problems of urban safety and victimization to set out policies and priorities based on partnership consensus.

- Development of local action plans that address the causes of crime and victimization, not just its symptoms.

- Implementation and evaluation of long- and short-term prevention projects that target social exclusion and urban poverty as well as specific crimes and specific geographical areas.

- Understanding that community crime prevention is a long-term process which requires educating the community that prevention is a normal part of local community activity and local governance.

The range of agencies, organizations, and individuals who should be involved in this process is very extensive, offering considerable flexibility and opportunities. A list of potential partners for developing a comprehensive plan was developed by NCPC (Kelly, 1998). The list includes

- Local government leadership.

- Law enforcement and criminal justice agencies.

- Human and social service agencies.

- Neighborhood and civic associations and clubs.

- Youth and seniors groups.

- Health, safety, and quality-of-life agencies.

- Universities, schools, school boards, principals, and Parent Teacher Associations.

- Cultural and ethnic populations.

- Business owners and organizations.

- Faith community leaders.

- Local media.

- Nonprofit groups.

- Public housing residents associations and management.

- Military.

IV. Limitations, Lessons, and Conclusions

This chapter provides examples of the ways in which different cities and local governments around the world have applied the community safety approach. Because a great deal can be learned from program failure, the chapter examines limitations and lessons that have been learned from past experience in developing community safety initiatives and local partnerships. Some of the most important lessons for developing partnerships, undertaking safety audits, and developing strategies and programs come from learning what went wrong, what proved to be difficult, and what went right.

> WE SHOULD STOP THINKING ABOUT COMMUNITIES AS HOMOGENOUS NEIGHBOURHOODS AND START RECOGNIZING THAT THEY COMPRISE INTEREST GROUPS THAT ARE OFTEN IN CONFLICT.
>
> —"Participatory Policing," *Imbizo*

Two important and related discussions of the past few years have revolved around what we mean when we talk about "community" and whether local authorities are really able to work with all members of a neighborhood. At the heart of these discussions are the following realities:

- Conflicts need to be talked through, not smoothed over.

- It is easier to work with established members than to include marginal groups.

- Communities that are weakest need the most help and support.

- Cities and local authorities must be willing to share the blame and the credit.

Having the tools to promote community safety is not enough. Also needed is clear understanding of the underlying problem. It is important to resist focusing only on the symptoms of crime and disorder in a community, or only on visible crime in public places. Minority groups, for example, may be wary of reporting harassment or crime. Recognizing the long-term nature of community change, and working on the process itself, may be more important than focusing on projects, current fads, or quick results.

Partnership Problems and Information Sharing

Developing partnerships is not easy and requires the following:

- Getting agencies to work together and share information.

- Ensuring that some agencies, such as the police, do not dominate.

- Ensuring that community partnerships represent the interests of the minority as well as the majority.

- Ensuring that women and men have an equal voice.

- Maintaining confidentiality during information-sharing efforts.

- Retaining momentum and sustaining initiatives.

Problems may arise when partners have different management styles, volunteers and paid staff try to work together, and leaders change.

Differences in Management Styles

Salt Lake City's experience developing Community Action Teams (CATs) revealed a number of management-generated problems (Rosenbaum, 1999). Tensions arose between city departments with different management styles. The open management style of the mayor's office that encouraged brainstorming, cooperative problem solving, and risk taking was in conflict with the traditional hierarchical and bureaucratic style of the city police department. As a result, some local CATs identified more with their community than with the city because the management of the teams had not been clearly thought through. This situation led to the isolation of CAT police officers from their colleagues and was only resolved when the police department made organizational and communication changes. In addition, community residents initially were not recruited as regular members of CAT because of the confidentiality of information being shared, while other team members, such as community prosecutors, attended meetings irregularly.

Volunteer Groups and Multiagency Work

Multiagency local partnerships to reduce domestic violence have been encouraged in several countries over the past 10 years. Experience has shown that such partnerships have many benefits but present difficulties (Hague, 1999). Volunteer groups tend to be underrepresented in such partnerships, while agency groups tend to assert control. Partnerships can pose problems for grassroots organizations that want to retain their independence as service providers. Long-established organizations providing services to women can be ignored in the rush to develop "new" initiatives. Women who have experienced domestic violence often have their needs and

Limitations, Lessons, and Conclusions

views overlooked. Small minority groups can be marginalized by local partnerships, whose membership often does not reflect the diversity of the community.

> WE BELIEVE THAT THE ROAD TO SUCCESS-
> FUL IMPLEMENTATION LIES NOT IN RUNNING
> AWAY FROM THE CONCEPT OF "COMMUNITY"
> BUT IN EMBRACING IT, STUDYING IT,
> UNDERSTANDING IT, AND RESPONDING TO IT
> APPROPRIATELY.
>
> —*The Prevention of Crime*

Changing Leaders

Sustaining initiatives is difficult when mayors or police chiefs are replaced, when funding runs out, or other priorities dominate. In Toronto, for example, a new mayor was elected as the task force on community safety submitted its plan. Responsibility for implementing the plan was not given to the office of the chief administrator as the task force had recommended, but to a different agency as part of the city's reorganization, one with a number of other functions. Over time, staff changes resulted in a loss of institutional memory, making it difficult for the implementers to generate and sustain the energy, time, and resources needed to realize the plan. A lesson to be learned from many initiatives is that they need to be supported by both a "champion" and community members who feel that they own part of the process and who will maintain momentum as elected officials or leaders move on.

Evaluation and Funding Issues

Projects can be evaluated at different stages: Have they met immediate, short-term, or long-term goals and are they cost effective? Some researchers have emphasized the importance of looking at the process of program development and implementation rather than just the outcome in terms of reductions in crime. What were the conditions that helped the program work or fail? It is clear that the more multidisciplinary and comprehensive a program, the more difficult it is to assess exactly what worked. What is important is to establish a range of short- and long-term goals and outcomes for projects.

While creatively using existing funds and resources and bringing together untapped energy is part of the new way of working, funding is still important. Unfortunately it is still categorically driven in many countries and tied to particular problems or initiatives. A pooling of resources is more valuable for city initiatives or community contracts that fund local prevention councils to develop a range of projects that meet their needs. In a number of countries, business partners support and sponsor projects, but continued funding is not always easy to obtain on a long-term basis.

Emerging Issues

A public health approach to community safety that looks at risk factors is valuable, but it is also important to look at the strengths and assets of individuals and communities. Other issues that need to be considered include the role of volunteers and faith communities and how they can best be included under local government leadership; the extent to which public groups can intervene in private issues or private locations; the rights of young people to public space; and the impact of new technologies on communities.

In Europe, new jobs associated with community safety, such as mediation and security assistants, outreach workers, youth wardens, community safety officers, and mediators, are showing promise. Communication technologies, especially the Internet, offer opportunities for exchanging experiences and expertise, training, and linking municipalities together.

Centralized States and Federal Nations

The different approaches to facilitating local government involvement in community safety show similarities and pose questions. It seems clear that local action needs to be supported vertically as well as horizontally. Netherlands, Belgium, England, and Wales, for example, have leaders at the national level linked to regional and local municipal leaders. While regions or counties adapt and develop community programs to meet their needs, there are binding requirements and, in some cases, legislation attached to funding contracts that require them to act in partnerships.

In France, the interministerial delegation to the city (DIV) requires all sectors—health, justice, housing, employment—to work together to develop the economic and social health of cities. The cities are able to define their own alliances in relation to their own needs. This gives them legitimacy and allows them to negotiate, innovate, and modify the functions of local agencies and develop new capacities.

Australia and Canada, federal countries with national structures, are not able to mandate their provinces, territories, or states with such ease. Nevertheless, their national crime prevention centers are well placed to offer funding, stimulate best practices, and coordinate information to regional and local groups. The United States, with a federal structure but strong state autonomy, arguably has less leverage to enforce or legislate. It has, nevertheless, managed to encourage a considerable amount of important locally based action across communities, enabling mayors, elected representatives, city managers, and administrators to make links with their regions and states as well as with federal funders.

Limitations, Lessons, and Conclusions

Summary

The pace of change in cities around the world has increased enormously in the past few years:

- With rapid globalization, urbanization, and migration, the health and well-being of citizens are major concerns in developed and developing countries.

- Poverty and exclusion, two of the most important problems facing cities and municipalities, have increased and are major factors increasing the risks of crime, victimization, and insecurity.

- In the past decades, despite tougher criminal justice responses in many countries, the problems of community safety have increased and remain a major concern for citizens.

- There has been a loss of faith in criminal justice systems.

- There has been recognition of the importance of prevention and of community safety as a right, and recognition of the need to revitalize cities and municipalities to deal with the social exclusion of young people and their families.

Since the 1980s, mayors and other local authority leaders have begun to promote community safety. They no longer see crime as primarily the responsibility of the police. They have come to see crime reduction as an issue of good governance that requires community partnerships to tailor local solutions to local problems. Accumulating evidence from many countries points to similarities in the factors that place people and places at risk of crime and victimization, the most important factors being poverty and discrimination. Evidence of the short- and long-term effectiveness of intervention to reduce risks is also accumulating and has been shown to be cost effective.

V. Examples From Practice

This chapter highlights a variety of community safety initiatives developed by local government partnerships in countries around the world. They have been selected to illustrate different aspects of the strategic approach and to show how communities of different sizes have tackled a range of issues. The initiatives include strategic plans in large cities following safety audits and public consultation; neighborhood-based committees and action groups; urban planning and management strategies for youth and public spaces; small-town initiatives; domestic violence strategies; statewide city initiatives targeting hotspots and cooperative financing; coalitions of local authorities and cities; and social observatories as tools for strategic local planning.[18]

Borough of Brent, London, England: Community Safety and Community Empowerment

Brent is one of 33 London boroughs, each with its own mayor and council. Brent has a population of 240,000 and the highest proportion (50 percent) of black and ethnic minority citizens in London. It is the most culturally and racially diverse of all local authorities in England and Wales and includes areas of considerable wealth and extreme poverty. The borough's average unemployment rate is 13 percent but runs as high as 30 percent in some wards. Crime rates in the borough are higher than the national average and are concentrated in deprived housing estates, some of which present serious policing problems. Major concerns are street robbery, theft and burglary, drug- and alcohol-related crime, and violence.

Working Partnership

Brent now has 10 years of experience working with partnerships, undertaking safety diagnoses, and planning and implementing community safety strategies. It has a permanent department of Community Safety and Community

> In Brent's experience the three key principles necessary for effective local authority crime prevention work can be classified as the three C's:
>
> - *Councillors:* to secure political support for crime prevention.
>
> - *Corporate:* to secure a council corporate approach to crime prevention.
>
> - *Coalitions:* to ensure that local authorities take the lead in developing crime prevention strategies.
>
> —John Blackmore, Head of Community Safety and Community Empowerment, Borough of Brent

Empowerment within its Community Development Directorate, which works closely with all council services, national agencies, and businesses.

Brent has five interagency crime prevention/community safety strategies. Projects developed with partners have included burglary reduction programs, a mentoring scheme for young people, neighborhood watch, and a targeted policing initiative for high-crime areas using crime mapping and analysis. The latter has been funded by a £1.3 million national government grant.

Brent has also set up accredited community safety training courses for local citizens and a community information system Web site (www.brent.gov.uk/brain). The borough recently held a conference on community safety that was transmitted on the Internet and will form the basis of a video. Its safety strategy for 1999– 2002, which followed a safety audit and extensive community consultation, was produced by the partnership between the local council and the police, probation service, and health authorities serving the borough.

The Crime and Disorder Audit compared Brent's crime levels with neighboring boroughs, highlighted crime hotspots, and examined trends in burglary, robbery, violence, sexual offenses, young offenders, domestic violence, racial incidents, victimization of the elderly, disorder, road injuries, drug and alcohol problems, and fear of crime. It showed that between 1996 and 1998, recorded crime had decreased in the borough by 5 percent, burglary had decreased by 13 percent, and street robbery had decreased by 14 percent, although violent crimes as a whole had risen. The audit listed some of the options for reducing the problems identified.

Community Safety Strategy for Brent 1999–2002

Top priorities:

1. Reduce residential burglary.

2. Decrease robbery and street-crime.

3. Improve partnership response to racial incidents and violence and victimization of ethnic minorities.

4. Reduce crime and disorder in town centers.

5. Reduce crime by young offenders.

Community Consultation

Some 10,000 copies of a summary of the crime and disorder audit were sent to the public and to ethnic minority, faith, neighborhood watch, and business groups. The full audit was available in police stations, libraries, and medical clinics. Forums were held to discuss the audit with resident and tenant organizations, police community consultation groups, and the Brent Youth Council.

The resulting document, *A Crime and Disorder Reduction and Community Safety Strategy for Brent 1999–2002* (Borough of Brent, 2000), identifies the borough's 15 priority targets, an overall target for each priority, a detailed list of action plans for each target, and performance measures to assess their effectiveness. The top priority is burglary reduction and the target is reduction by a minimum of 6 percent in 12 months, or 12 percent in 36 months, compared with 1998 figures. Apart from the top five priorities listed on page 36, other priority targets include reducing youth victimization, domestic violence, road injuries, and drug and alcohol abuse.

Contact: John Blackmore, Head, Community Safety and Community Empowerment, London Borough of Brent, Brent Town Hall, Forty Lane, Wembley, Middlesex, HA9 9HD, England. 44–020–8937–1035; 44–020–8937–1056 (fax); john.blackmore@brent.gov.uk (e-mail).

Toronto, Ontario, Canada: A Community Safety Strategy for the City

Toronto, with a population 2.5 million, has seen enormous growth as a city and region over the past 20 years. This growth includes rapid changes in the ethnic distribution of the population. Before 1980, 60 percent of immigrants were from Europe. Since 1980, the majority of immigrants have come from Asia, Africa, Latin America, the Caribbean, China, Hong Kong, and the Philippines. About 42 percent of citizens have a mother tongue other than English. These changes have brought considerable social and economic benefits, but there is increasing income disparity and poverty. Only 27 to 36 percent of Toronto citizens feel that all ethnic and cultural groups are treated fairly by city politicians and the police. Violent crime levels were still increasing as recently as 1997, and community safety remains one of citizens' top concerns.

Formerly a city of 650,000, the new megacity of Toronto was created in 1998 with the amalgamation of the surrounding municipalities of East York, Etobicoke, North York, Scarborough, and York. The new city council established a Task Force on Community Safety to develop a comprehensive safety plan. Chaired by two councillors, it included representatives from the police, school boards, neighborhood crime prevention groups, businesses, ethno-cultural groups and agencies, organizations working with at-risk children and people with disabilities, and family violence counselors.

Its key strategy was community consultation using a community survey, interviews with city councillors, public meetings, and presentations.

Toronto Community Safety Strategy

A Vision for a Safer City

- Reduce crime and fear of crime.
- Increase community knowledge and involvement in creating a safer city.
- Focus on vulnerable groups.
- Recognize diversity.
- Know what works and the importance of evaluation.

Five Directions for Action

- Strengthen neighborhoods.
- Invest in children and youth.
- Increase police and justice.
- Obtain information and organize coordination.
- Make community safety a corporate policy with a council accountability structure.

Its interim report was discussed at a conference bringing together citizens, local organizations, and councillors.

The final report *Toronto, My City, A Safe City: A Community Strategy for the City of Toronto* (1999), outlines the extent of the city's problems of crime, insecurity, and inequalities. It discusses their root causes and how they can be overcome, describes existing community services and programs, sets out its vision for a safe city within a healthy communities framework, and outlines 35 recommendations for implementation. Each recommendation identifies the major city services that should take the lead. A new task force was established in 2000 to develop a work plan to implement the recommendations. Among other work, a social atlas, based on analysis of city wards, is being constructed and implementation of the plan is expected to take 3 years.

Contact: Lydia Fitchko, Policy Development Officer, City of Toronto Community and Neighborhood Services Department, Social Development and Administration Division, 55 John Street, 11th Floor Metro Hall, Toronto, Ontario M5V 3C6, Canada. 416-392-5397; 416-392-8492 (fax); lfitchko@city.toronto.on.ca (e-mail).

Brisbane, Queensland, Australia: Youth and Public Space Major Centers Project

Brisbane is a major Australian city with a population of 1.6 million and regional and subregional satellite centers. Recently, it has experienced a strong population growth, including immigration from Southeast Asia. Crime, vandalism, incivilities in public places, the presence of street kids and youth gangs, and the increasing exclusion of minority youth are major concerns.

High numbers of indigenous young people have migrated from rural areas and the city suffers from a lack of transport, social services, and facilities designed to meet the needs of young people.

Examples From Practice

Brisbane began a project to develop safer public spaces that were more inclusive and relevant to the needs and interests of young people. It focused on the major public sites where young people gathered, such as city and regional shopping malls, beaches, and parks. The project took as its starting point the importance of recognizing the inherent right of young people to have access to public spaces and to be consulted and involved in the development of facilities.

> A CRUCIAL ISSUE IS WHETHER YOUNG PEOPLE VIEW AMENITIES AS YOUTH FRIENDLY. A SURVEY OF YOUNG PEOPLE FOUND THAT THE FACTORS INVOLVED IN DEFINING A PLACE AS 'FRIENDLY' INCLUDED ACCEPTANCE AND SUPPORT, NO VIOLENCE, CHEAP FOOD AND DRINKS, AND NO ADULTS OR POLICE.
>
> —*Hanging Out: Negotiating Young People's Use of Public Space*

The city held extensive discussions with young people and other users of commercial and community spaces and compiled information on the city council strategic planning system, corporate and local area plans, and urban design. It examined good practice models and principles and the current use of major centers in the city, suburbs, and regions. It set out principles, recommended policies, detailed strategy outlines, and targeted indicators to reach each of the policy objectives in three areas: youth and community development policy, urban management through strategic and local planning and design, and operational management and community relations in major centers.

A related project, Girls in Space Consortia (1997), looked at the needs of girls and young women in public spaces. Brisbane now has good examples of well planned and designed city centers such as Southbank.

Youth and Community Development Policy Principles

- Inclusive public and community spaces.
- Recognizing the tension between commercial and community objectives.
- Understanding shopping centers in their local and regional contexts.
- Active inclusion of young people.
- Responsive and coordinated policy development within the council.
- Promoting realistic and accurate information on young people to the broader community.
- Responding to diversity among young people.
- Safety.

—*Hanging Out: Negotiating Young People's Use of Public Space*

Source: P. Haywood, P. Crane, A. Egginton, and J. Gleeson (1998), *Out and About: In or Out? Better Outcomes for Young People's Use of Public and Community Space in the City of Brisbane.*

Leichhardt Municipal Council, New South Wales, Australia: Draft Youth Social Plan

This small municipal council, serving a population of 62,053, developed its Youth Social Plan 1995–1997 (White, 1998) to respond to local unemployment, poverty, and inequality to provide concrete ways of dealing with current problems. These included conflicts over the use of public space by young people. The plan asserts the basic rights of young people and outlines strategies for the following:

- Area planning and local services coordination.

- More equitable distribution of youth services and facilities throughout the municipality.

- Youth consultation, participation, and advocacy.

- Recreation and public space provision for young people.

- Youth facilities for commercial developments.

- Active recreational spaces.

- Public space design and inclusion of artwork.

- Health and well-being of young people.

- Youth and family support services.

- Education, training, and employment.

- Housing and homelessness.

- Crime prevention.

Source: "The Youth Section of Leichhardt Municipal Council's Draft Social Plan 1997–1999: Defining How Council Works With and on Behalf of Young People Aged 12–24." R. White (1998), *Public Spaces for Young People.*

Freeport, Illinois: Coalition for a Safe Community

In the early 1990s, 25 percent of Freeport's 27,000 citizens lived at or below the poverty line, with 54 percent of children living in poverty. African Americans made up 20 percent of the population and there were concerns about disparities in educational provision and treatment of students.

The catalyst to action was a threat by four Fortune 500 companies, which provided 40 percent of local employment, to pull out of the city. The city set up Project 2009 with local businesses in 1993. They developed a strategic plan to ensure that 90 percent of young people stayed in school and graduated equipped to work in local businesses. The project coalition included city leaders, school administrators, business and community representatives, and local clergy.

Beginning in 1994, the mayor met with residents over the course of 18 months to discuss and debate concerns about increasing violence. In 1996, the city established the Coalition for a Safe Community, whose mission was to build a safe and healthy community for children and families. Four task forces developed plans leading to the creation of family mentoring, parenting education, media awareness programs, and a job bank.

The results have been significant. Rates of child abuse and neglect have fallen. The local newspaper has developed a guide to local family and social services. New lighting has been installed. A new neighborhood park and play area is planned. School buildings are now available as community centers, and 50 new mentors for local youth are being recruited by local organizations and businesses. Even with a new mayor and police chief, in 1997 and 1998, implementation of the plan was completed. The coalition has obtained more than $450,000 from federal, state, and foundation grants and plans to develop an affordable housing project.

Contact: Tracey Johnson, Deputy Director, MLKCSI, 511 South Liberty Street, Freeport, IL 61032. 815–233–9915; 815–235–0007 (fax).

Hartford, Connecticut: Neighborhood Problem-Solving Committees and the Comprehensive Communities Program

From 1986 to 1996, severe neighborhood gang wars catapulted Hartford's crime levels into the top 10 for cities with more than 100,000 citizens. A mayor's commission on crime was set up in 1987. The commission recommended establishing citywide community policing, developing interagency partnerships, and combining community efforts to work on social issues.

A Police Gang Task Force was established in 1992, and neighborhood problem-solving committees (PSCs) were set up in the 17 city neighborhoods. PSCs meet monthly to diagnose neighborhood problems and decide on objectives and plans. Three special assistants to the city manager were hired to serve as liaisons between PSCs and the city government. Our Piece of the Pie, a prework program for youth, was set up in 1996. The program also began hiring young adults as trainers, counselors, and role models to support at-risk youth and set up a youth job clearinghouse. As a result of these efforts, overall rates of crime fell by 30 percent from 1986 to 1996, and rates of employment placement from the program have been up to 87 percent.

Contact: Rae Ann Palmer, Coordinator, Special Projects and Community Programs, City of Hartford, City Manager's Office, 525 Main Street, Hartford, CT 06103. 860-543-8681; 860-722-6216 (fax).

Salt Lake City, Utah: Changing the Way Government Works and the Comprehensive Communities Program

In recent years, Salt Lake City has not only grown in population but become increasingly diverse ethnically and racially as well. Youth violence, including drive-by shootings, and gang-related crime rose in the early 1990s. At that time, the percentage of the city's 180,000 people living below the poverty level was 16.4 percent, compared with the national average of 12.8 percent. In 1995, its unemployment rate was 3.6 percent, compared with the national average of 5.6 percent, and the rate of violent crime was 83 per 10,000, compared with the national level of 72 per 10,000. Fear of crime increased and the courts were overloaded.

The city set up Community Action Teams (CATs) in each geographical area, as neighborhood-based problem-solving teams focusing on the problems of youth and youth gangs. CATs include community police, probation, the city prosecutor, community mobilization specialists, a youth/family specialist, and a community relations coordinator. CAT youth workers from the local Boys & Girls Club help link at-risk youth to local services. More recently, school representatives have joined each team. CATs meet weekly to deal with neighborhood problems, with the aim of providing services quickly to clients, cutting across agency boundaries and red tape. The mayor's Office of Community Affairs acts as the liaison between agencies and city government and the teams.

THE PURPOSE OF COMMUNITY ACTION TEAMS IS TO POOL THEIR RESOURCES (TIME, AUTHORITY, STAFF) IN A PROBLEM-SOLVING FOCUS ON NEIGHBORHOOD-SPECIFIC AND FAMILY-SPECIFIC PROBLEMS AS THEY ARISE.... CATS ARE EMPOWERED BY UPPER-LEVEL CITY MANAGEMENT TO WORK OUT THE MOST EFFECTIVE SOLUTION THEY CAN DEVISE THROUGH COLLABORATION AMONG MEMBER AGENCIES AND THE COMMUNITY.

—*Standing In the Gap*

Some of the outcomes of Salt Lake City's approach include Community Peace Services, a diversion program that provides education, mediation, and intervention to first-time offenders; a domestic violence court; and increased youth and family specialist staff. The city has been able to attract increased resources from federal, state, and local government and from foundations. These have led to new programs and new staff. Gang activity has diminished, property crime is down, and homicides have declined 33 percent from 1995.

Contact: Jeanne Robinson, Assistant City Prosecutor, Salt Lake City. 801–535–7660.

Maryland HotSpot Communities: Reclaiming Our Neighborhoods

This initiative targets heavy concentrations of crime, insecurity, and victimization in 36 HotSpot communities across Maryland. The effort began in 1997 and provides funds to neighborhoods to develop partnerships and strategies to reclaim those areas. The program recognizes that nationally 50 percent of crime occurs at 3 percent of addresses. It is the first statewide intervention to help selected HotSpot areas reclaim their neighborhoods, investing $3.5 million in state and federal grant funding in 36 communities.

A major innovation of the initiative is coordinating state and federal funding to support "core" and "enhancing" projects arising from strategic plans. Each community receives operational and technical assistance from various state and local agencies. The core elements are community mobilization, community policing, community probation, community maintenance, crime prevention among youth, and local coordination. The enhancing elements are community prosecution, juvenile intervention, crime prevention through environmental design, victim outreach and assistance, community support for addiction recovery, and housing and business revitalization.

Contact: Stephen Amos, Executive Director, Governor's Office of Crime Control and Prevention, 300 East Joppa Road, Suite 1105, Baltimore, MD 21286–3016. 410–321–3521; 410–321–3116 (fax); STEPHEN@GOCCP-State-MD.org (e-mail).

METRAC, Toronto, Ontario, Canada: Taking Action Against Abuse of Women

One in 6 women in Canada is abused by her partner each year and more than 60 percent of homicides result from family violence. A major problem in Canada has been the lack of coordination of services and programs across all sectors.

Sponsored by the chair of Metro Toronto in 1992, the Metro Woman Abuse Council of Toronto was formed to create a metrowide integrated community response to violence against women that promotes effective and efficient provision of services for assaulted women and their families. The city provides in-kind support. The council brings together 18 representatives of key sectors of the community, including shelters, police departments, hospitals, support service agencies, community health centers, probation officers, and survivor groups. There are five standing committees and ad hoc working groups.

The council's successes include conferences that have brought together different sectors and groups, two publications (*Best Practice Resource Manual* and *Best Practice Guidelines for Responding to Women Abuse for Health Practitioners*), safety audit kits, protocols and accountability standards for intervention programs, and education and awareness projects. The council worked with police departments and courts to develop specialized domestic violence courts, model batterer's programs, and court-watch projects, and developed inter-sectoral partnerships and protocols.

Contact: www.city.toronto.on.ca/council/wac_index.htm#f (Internet).

Amsterdam, The Hague, Rotterdam, and Utrecht, Netherlands: Big Cities Policy

Social problems such as drugs, nuisance, and street crime in Netherlands' major cities led to the development of a Big Cities Policy. A memorandum was drawn up by the municipal authorities of the major cities to strengthen their social and economic bases in partnership with the national government in three major areas: employment and education, public safety, and quality of life and care. The main impact is directed at the neighborhood level and the plan sets targets and outlines measures.

As part of the initiative, a pilot project modeled on the French example, Justice in the Neighborhood: Justice Closer to the Citizens and Their Problems, was begun in 1992.[19] Neighborhood justice offices were opened in five Dutch cities to work in problem-oriented ways with local residents. The offices provide accessible, quick, and direct action to deal with local street crime, nuisances, and conflicts. They offer information, legal advice, and conflict mediation to help prevent local disputes from getting out of control.

Contact: Ministry of Justice, Information Department, 31-0-70-370-68-50; 31-0-70-370-75-94 (fax); infodesk@wodc.minjust.nl or voorlichting@best-dep.minjust.nl (e-mail); www.minjust.nl:8080 (Internet).

EURO 2000 Football Cities Against Racism

The European Forum for Urban Safety funds groups of cities in Europe to tackle specific problems. Over the past 10 years it has brought member cities together for conferences and initiatives on violence and schools, the mass media, senior citizens, victims, immigration and insecurity, the integration of young people, and drug prevention. A recent initiative targets racism and soccer violence. Soccer violence has been a major problem in Great Britain as well as other European countries for a number of years. Nine host cities (Brent in London, four Dutch cities, and four Belgian cities) have developed antiracism campaigns around the EURO 2000 championships.

Contacts: John Blackmore, Head, Community Safety and Community Empowerment, London Borough of Brent, Brent Town Hall, Forty Lane, Wembley, Middlesex, HA9 9HD, England. 44–020–8937–1035; 44–020–8937–1056 (fax); john.blackmore@brent.gov.uk (e-mail); European Forum for Urban Safety, 38 rue Liancourt, Paris 75014, France. 33–1–40–64–49–00; 33–1–40–64–49–10 (fax); fesu@urbansecurity.org. (e-mail).

Aix en Provence, France: Local Security Contract and Observatory

This city of 126,000 has experienced considerable growth in the past 30 years. It is "rich, cultured, and young," but with increasing disparities between its economically stable and marginalized populations.

The city received a Contrat de Ville in 1994 to improve housing, transport, education, and health services, as well as to develop delinquency and drug prevention strategies. A community council partnership for the prevention of delinquency was formed that applied for a new security contract (CLS) as soon as they were announced in 1997. The partnership includes not only the city of Aix en Provence but its surrounding communities, each with its own mayor, police department, and other services. Representatives of the region and national ministries are also included.

A comprehensive security diagnosis was undertaken, looking at direct and indirect problems. In addition, a permanent observatory of social problems was created, using specific indicators at the local government level.

Using this knowledge as a foundation, the city established 10 priorities relating to the quality of life: social, cultural, and sports facilities and policies; citizen access to the law; prevention of child abuse and neglect; prevention of substance abuse; parental support; victim support and aid; improving court and reintegration policy and practices; and safety and security. The action plan (*Fiches actions de contrat*, 1999) outlines 42 separate actions relating to these 10 priorities. In each case it identifies the specific problem, the objectives set, the agreed action, the partners responsible for implementation, methods of finance, evaluation, and target dates. The prevention of school violence, for example, involves measures to reduce absenteeism and school exclusion, early identification of behavior problems, use of alternative disciplinary measures, and educational support. The plan is now being implemented and evaluated.

Among other initiatives, community policing has been established, and new security assistants have been recruited. Better links and coordination between the national and municipal police have also been set up. Social mediation agents have been recruited and trained to work on public transport, around schools, and in public spaces. Their role includes mediating situations and intervening between groups such as local shop owners and young people to try to develop creative solutions to problems. Although the outcomes have not yet been evaluated, the CLS has had a considerable impact on policies and practices in the city as well as the region.

Sources: Diagnostic local de securite de la Ville de Aix en Provence (1999) and Fiches actions de contrat (1999): Centre de gestion de la fonction publique territoriale des Bouches du Rhone.

VI. Notes

1. This statement refers to crimes recorded by the police. We know from victimization surveys taken in many countries that only approximately 50 percent of crime events are reported to the police, so these levels underestimate the extent of crime and victimization.

2. In England and Wales, for example, 59 percent of the public thought that crime rates were still rising in 1998 in spite of 4 years of decline (Mattinson and Mirrlees-Black, 2000).

3. For example, in Britain 82 percent of Pakistani and 84 percent of Bangladeshi families, many of them living in public housing, have incomes that are less than half the national average, compared with 28 percent of the majority white population (Social Exclusion Unit, 2000a: 30). In France, concentrations of social problems are found in the satellite housing complexes around the major cities with social outcasts and immigrant families living in far greater poverty and substandard conditions than the rest of the country (Dubet and Lapeyronnie, 1994, in Pfeiffer, 1998). In Germany, 39 percent of foreign born Turkish youth experience high levels of deprivation compared with 12 percent of native-born Germans (Pfeiffer and Wetzels, 1999).

4. See Snyder and Sickmund (1999) and Harris and Curtis (1998) for more information about juvenile offending and victimization and future population trends. Hagan (1996) and Rose and Clear (1998) have discussed the impact of high rates of imprisonment on neighborhoods.

5. An international survey in 12 countries found drug use was prevalent among youth in areas of high unemployment and was associated with a high incidence of property and violent crime (Killias and Ribeaud, 1999).

6. See *Violence Against Women: The Hidden Health Burden* (Heise, L.L., et al., 1994).

7. In Germany, for example, the proportion of ethnic minorities in youth custody increased from 10 percent in 1990 to 35 percent by 1998 (Pfeiffer and Wetzels, 1999).

8. These projects include summer holiday and job creation programs for disadvantaged young people. Since 1989 these city contracts have been administered through an interministerial agency (DIV) at the national level that links the interests of national ministries together in supporting a range of city projects.

9. Countries in transition include many east European countries that were part of the Soviet Union or the Eastern Bloc. Developing countries include many in South America, Africa, and Asia. International victimization surveys have been carried out in many of these countries since the mid-1990s.

10. These are being funded by the United Nations Center for Human Settlements (Habitat) based in Nairobi in partnership with ICPC, EFUS, the South African Institute of Security Studies, and national and local governments. Projects under the Habitat program are being developed in other African cities as well as in Asia and Latin America (www.unchs.org/safercities). The project in Dar es Salaam was awarded the Urban Security Prize at the Africities Summit 2000.

11. A safety audit includes a detailed mapping of crime and disorder problems in a community.

12. The National Strategy for Neighborhood Renewal is a multiministerial strategy for tackling the problems of deprived neighborhoods. Each of the 18 reports focuses on a particular issue. For example, Report 12 deals with young people (Social Exclusion Unit, 1999b); Report 4 with neighborhood renewal (Social Exclusion Unit, 2000a). Three major funding areas target crime reduction and community safety: Sure Start funds early family intervention programs, On Track funds projects for children and families, and Youth Include provides activities for at-risk youth between 13 and 16 years old.

13. See *Profils, Missions et Perspectives des Agents Locaux de Mediation Sociale* (Forum Francais, 1999).

14. These were the mayors of Arlington, Austin, Corpus Christi, Dallas, El Paso, Fort Worth, Houston, and San Antonio.

15. The sites in Baltimore, Boston, Columbia, Fort Worth, Salt Lake City, and Seattle have been intensively evaluated; Atlanta, Denver, East Bay, Hartford, and Wichita have been the subject of less intensive evaluation (Kelling et al., 1998). A total of $34 million was invested in the program.

16. They include Burlington, Chapel Hill, and Garner in North Carolina; Deerfield Park, Florida; Deer Park, Texas; Lima and Stow, Ohio; Keene, New Hampshire; Bessemer, Alabama; Pearl, Mississippi; and Pueblo County, Colorado.

17. The National Crime Prevention Council has produced a number of other guides to community initiatives in crime prevention, including *Crime Prevention in America: Foundations for Action* (1990); *Uniting Communities Through Crime Prevention* (1994); *New Ways of Working To Reduce Crime* (1996); and *Designing Safer Communities* (1997).

18. Other examples can be found in *100 Crime Prevention Programs To Inspire Action Across the World* (International Centre for the Prevention of Crime, 1999b).

19. Maisons de justice et du droit.

VII. References

Bonnemaison, G. (1982). *Rapport de la Commission des Maires sur la Sécurité*. Paris, France.

Borough of Brent (2000). *A Crime and Disorder Reduction and Community Safety Strategy for Brent 1999–2002*. London, England: Borough of Brent.

Bureau of Justice Assistance (1997). *Innovation State and Local Practices*. Washington, DC: U.S. Department of Justice.

Center for the Study and Prevention of Violence (1997). *Blueprints for Violence Prevention*. Boulder, CO: Center for the Study and Prevention of Violence.

Crime Concern (1998). *Reducing Neighbourhood Crime: A Manual for Action*. Swindon, England: Crime Concern.

Crime Concern (1999). *Review to Support the Development of the Health Strategy for London Crime and Disorder*. Woking, England: Crime Concern.

European Forum for Urban Safety (1996). *Tools for Action. Interim Report*. Paris, France: European Forum for Urban Safety.

European Forum for Urban Safety (1996). *Safety and Security: New Jobs for the New Millenium*. Paris, France: European Forum for Urban Safety.

Farrington, D.P. (2000). "Explaining and Preventing Crime." *Criminology* 38(1): 1–24.

Federal Bureau of Investigation (2000). *Preliminary Annual Uniform Crime Report, 1999*. Washington, DC: U.S. Department of Justice.

Hagan, J. (1996). "The Next Generation: Children of Prisoners." *The Unintended Consequences of Incarceration*. New York, NY: Vera Institute of Justice.

Hague, G. (1999). "Reducing Domestic Violence—What Works? Multi-Agency Fora." *Briefing Note: Policing and Reducing Crime*. London, England: Home Office.

Hamilton, J. (1999). *Results Centred Evaluation of Safer Community Councils*. Wellington, New Zealand: Crime Prevention Unit, Department of the Prime Minister.

Harris, F.R., and Curtis, L.A. (1998). *Locked in the Poorhouse: Cities, Race and Poverty in the United States*. New York, NY: Rowman & Littlefield.

Heise, L.L., et al. (1994). *Violence Against Women: The Hidden Health Burden*. Washington, DC: World Bank.

Hosain, S. (1995). *Cutting Crime in Rural Areas*. Swindon, England: Crime Concern.

International Centre for the Prevention of Crime (1999a). *Crime Prevention Digest II*. Montreal, Canada: International Centre for the Prevention of Crime.

International Centre for the Prevention of Crime (1999b). *100 Crime Prevention Programs To Inspire Action Across the World*. Montreal: International Centre for the Prevention of Crime.

Institut des Hautes Études de la Sécurité Intérieure (1998). *Guide Pratique Pour les Contrats Locaux de Sécurité*. Paris, France: Institut des Hautes Études de la Sécurité Intérieure.

Institute for Security Studies (1999). *International Conference on Safer Communities*. Pretoria, South Africa: Institute for Security Studies.

Junger-Tas, J. (1997). *Jeugd en Gezin*. The Hague, Netherlands: Ministry of Justice.

Kelling, G., Hochberg, M.R., Kaminski, S.L., Rocheleau, A.M., Rosenbaum, D.P., Roth, J.A., and Skogan, W.G. (1998). *The Bureau of Justice Assistance Comprehensive Communities Program: A Preliminary Report*. Research in Brief. Washington, DC: National Institute of Justice.

Kelly, T. (1998). "Planning Brings Results: Comprehensive Blueprints for Community Safety." NCPC presentation to National Conference on Preventing Crime, November 1998. Washington, DC: National Crime Prevention Council.

Killias, M., and Ribeaud, D. (1999). "Drug Use Among Juveniles: An International Perspective." *Studies on Crime Prevention* 8(2): 189–207.

Loeber, R., and Farrington, D.P. (1998). *Serious and Violent Crime Offenders*. Thousand Oaks, CA: Sage Publications.

Marcus, M. (1995). *Faces of Justice and Poverty in the City*. Paris, France: European Forum for Urban Safety.

Mattinson, J., and Mirrlees-Black, C. (2000). *Attitudes to Crime and Criminal Justice: Findings From the 1998 British Crime Survey*. Research Findings No. 111. London, England: Home Office Research, Development and Statistics Directorate.

Mayhew, P., and van Dijk, J.J. (1997). *Criminal Victimization in Eleven Industrialized Countries*. The Hague, Netherlands: WODC.

National Center on Addiction and Substance Abuse at Columbia University (2000). CASA White Paper, *No Place to Hide: Rural 8th*

Graders Using Drugs, Drinking and Smoking at Higher Rates Than Urban 8th Graders. New York, NY: National Center on Addiction and Substance Abuse at Columbia University.

National Crime Prevention. (1999). *Hanging Out: Negotiating Young People's Use of Public Space*. Australian Capital Territory: National Crime Prevention, Attorney General's Department.

National Crime Prevention Council (1994). *Taking the Offensive to Prevent Crime: How Seven Cities Did It*. Washington, DC: National Crime Prevention Council.

National Crime Prevention Council (1998). *Creating a Blueprint for Community Safety: A Guide for Local Action*. Washington, DC: National Crime Prevention Council.

National Crime Prevention Council (1999a). *Six Safer Cities: On the Crest of the Crime Prevention Wave*. Washington DC: National Crime Prevention Council.

National Crime Prevention Council (1999b). *Standing in the Gap: Local Family Strengthening Initiatives for Safer, Better Communities*. Washington DC: National Crime Prevention Council.

National Crime Prevention Council (2000). *150 Tested Strategies To Prevent Crime From Small Cities, Counties, and Rural Communities*. Washington, DC: National Crime Prevention Council.

National League of Cities (1996). *Connecting Citizens and Their Government: Civility, Responsibility and Democracy*. Washington, DC: National League of Cities.

Nuttall, C.P., Goldblatt, P., and Lewis, C. (Eds.) (1998). *Reducing Offending: An Assessment of Research Evidence on Ways of Dealing With Offending Behavior*. Home Office Research Study No. 187. London, England: Home Office.

Pfeiffer, C. (1998). "Juvenile Crime and Violence in Europe." *Crime and Justice. A Review of Research* 23: 255–328. Chicago, IL: University of Chicago Press.

Pfeiffer, C., and Wetzels, P. (1999). *The Structure and Development of Juvenile Violence in Germany*. Forschungsberichte No. 76. Hanover, Germany: Kriminologisches Forschungsinstitut Niedersachsen.

Rose, D.R., and Clear, T.R. (1998). "Incarceration, Social Capital, and Crime." *Criminology* 36(3): 441–479.

Rosenbaum, D.P. (1999). "Creation of a Neighborhood-Based Government in Salt Lake City." Paper presented at the American Society of Criminology Annual Meeting. Toronto, Canada: November 17–20.

Rosenbaum, D.P., Lurigio, A.J., and Davis, R.C. (1998). *The*

Prevention of Crime: Social and Situational Strategies. Belmont, CA: Wadsworth Publishing Company.

Sarre, R. (1991). "Problems and Pitfalls in Crime Prevention." National Overview on Crime Prevention. Adelaide, Australia: Australian Institute of Criminology.

Shearing, C. (1994). "Participatory Policing," Imbizo 2: 5–10.

Sherman, L.W., Gottfredson, D., MacKenzie, D., Eck, J., Reuter, P., and Bushway, S. (1997). What Works, What Doesn't Work, What's Promising. Washington, DC: National Institute of Justice.

Snyder, H.N., and Sickmund, M. (1999). Juvenile Offenders and Victims: 1999 National Report. Washington, DC: Office of Juvenile Justice and Delinquency Prevention.

Social Exclusion Unit (1999a). Bridging the Gap. London, England: The Stationery Office.

Social Exclusion Unit (1999b). National Strategy for Neighbourhood Renewal Report of Policy Action Team 12: Young People. London, England: The Stationery Office.

Social Exclusion Unit (2000a). National Strategy for Neighbourhood Renewal Report of Policy Action Team 4: Neighbourhood Management. London, England: The Stationery Office.

Social Exclusion Unit (2000b). National Strategy for Neighbourhood Renewal Report of Policy Action Team 17: Joining It Up Locally. London, England: The Stationery Office.

van Zyl Smit, D. (1999). "Criminological Ideas and the South African Transition." British Journal of Criminology 39(2).

Waller, I., and Welsh, B. (1999). "International Trends in Crime Prevention: Cost-effective Ways To Reduce Victimization." Global Report on Crime and Justice. United Nations Office for Drug Control and Crime Prevention. New York, NY: Oxford University Press.

White, R. (1998). Public Spaces for Young People: A Guide to Creative Projects and Positive Strategies. New South Wales, Australia: Australian Youth Foundation and National Campaign Against Violence and Crime.

Wong, S., Catalano, R., Hawkins, J.D., and Chappell, P. (1996). Communities That Care Prevention Strategies: A Research Guide to What Works. Seattle, WA: Developmental Research & Programs, Inc.

VIII. Resources and Addresses

National Crime Prevention
(Australia)
Attorney General's Department
Robert Garran Offices
National Circuit
Barton Act 2600
Australia
61–02–6250–6711
Fax: 61–02–6273–0913
E-mail: commentsncp@ag.gov.au
Web site: www.ncp.gov.au

Australian Local Government
Association
8 Geils Court
Deakin Act 2600
Australia
61–02–6281–1211
Fax: 61–02–6282–2110
E-mail: alga@alga.com.au
Web site: www.alga.com.au

Secrétariat permanent à la politique
de prévention (Belgium)
Ministére de l'Intérieur
26, rue de la Loi bte 19
Brussels 1040
Belgique
32–2–500–49–47
Fax: 32–2–500–49–87
E-mail: info@belgium.fgov.be
Web site: www.vspp.fgov.be

International Centre for the
Prevention of Crime (Canada)
507, Place d'Armes, Suite 2100
Montreal, Quebec
H2Y 2W8
Canada
514–288–6731
Fax: 514–288–8763
E-mail:
 cipc@crime-prevention-intl.org
Web site: crime-prevention-intl.org

International Crime Prevention
Action Network (Canada)
BC Coalition for Safer Communities
c/o The People's Law School
605–318 Horner Street
Vancouver, British Columbia
V6B 2V2
Canada
604–669–2986
Fax: 604–689–2619
E-mail: icpan@web.ca
Web site: www.web.net/~icpan

National Crime Prevention Centre
(Canada)
Department of Justice of Canada
123 Slater Street
Ottawa, Ontario
K1A 0H8
Canada
877–302–CNPC (French);
877–302–NCPC (English)
Fax: 613–952–3515
E-mail: cnpc@web.net (French);
 ncpc@web.net (English)
Web site: www.crime-prevention.org

Crime Concern (England)
Beaver House
147–150 Victoria Road
Swindon Wiltshire SN1 3BU
England

Crime Prevention Agency
(England)
Home Office
50 Queen Anne's Gate
London SW1H 9AT
England
0171–273–3000
Fax: 0171–273–4037
E-mail: public.enquiries@
   homeoffice.gsi.gov.uk
Web site: www.homeoffice.gov.uk

Social Exclusion Unit (England)
Cabinet Office
35 Great Smith Street
London SW1P 3BQ
England
020–7276–2055 (general inquiries)
Fax: 020–7276–2056
E-mail:
   jowood@cabinetoffice.x.gsi.gov.uk
Web site:
   www.cabinet-office.gov.uk/seu

Délégation Interministérielle à la
Ville et au Développement Social
Urbain (France)
194, avenue du Président Wilson
St-Denis-La Plaine 93217
France
Tel: 33–1–49–17–46–10
Fax: 33–1–49–17–45–55
E-mail: didier.michal@ville.gouv.fr

European Forum for Urban Safety
(France)
38, rue Liancourt
75014 Paris
France
33–1–43–27–83–11
Fax: 33–1–43–27–79–52
Web site: www.urbansecurity.org

Secretariat for Safety and Security
(South Africa)
Private Bag X463
Pretoria 0001
South Africa
27–012–339–15–86
Fax: 27–012–339–25–36
E-mail: blfdoss@iafrica.com
Web site: www.gcis.gov.za/sss

Boys & Girls Clubs of America
(USA)
National Headquarters
1230 West Peachtree Street NW.
Atlanta, GA 30309–3447
1–800–854–CLUB
Web site: www.bgca.org

Bureau of Justice Assistance
(USA)
U.S. Department of Justice
810 Seventh Street NW.
Fourth Floor
Washington, DC 20531
202–616–6500
Fax: 202–305–1367
E-mail: askbja@ojp.usdoj.gov
Web site: www.ojp.usdoj.gov/BJA

Resources and Addresses

National Crime Prevention Council
1000 Connecticut Avenue NW.
Thirteenth Floor
Washington, DC 20036
202–466–6272
Fax: 202–296–1356
Web site: www.ncpc.org

National Funding Collaborative on Violence Prevention (USA)
815 15th Street NW.
Suite 801
Washington, DC 20005
202–393–7731
Fax: 202–393–4148
E-mail: lbowen@nfcvp.org
Web site: www.peacebeyondviolence.org

Office of Juvenile Justice and Delinquency Prevention (USA)
U.S. Department of Justice
810 Seventh Street NW.
Eighth Floor
Washington, DC 20531
202–307–5911
Fax: 202–307–2093
E-mail: ASKJJ@ojp.usdoj.gov
Web site: ojjdp.ncjrs.org

IX. For More Information

For information regarding the topics and programs discussed in this monograph, contact:

Margaret Shaw
Director, Analysis and Exchange
International Centre for the
  Prevention of Crime
507 Place d'Armes, Suite 2100
Montreal, Quebec
H2Y 2W8
Canada
514–288–6731, ext. 227
Fax: 514–288–8763
E-mail: shaw@crime-prevention-intl.org
Web site: www.crime-prevention-intl.org

For additional information on BJA grants and programs, contact:

Bureau of Justice Assistance
810 Seventh Street NW.
Fourth Floor
Washington, DC 20531
202–616–6500
Fax: 202–305–1367
Web site:
    www.ojp.usdoj.gov/BJA

Bureau of Justice Assistance Clearinghouse
P.O. Box 6000
Rockvile, MD 20849–6000
1–800–688–4252
Web site: www.ncjrs.org

Clearinghouse staff are available Monday through Friday, 8:30 a.m. to 7 p.m. eastern time. Ask to be placed on the BJA mailing list.

U.S. Department of Justice Response Center
1–800–421–6770 or 202–307–1480

Response Center staff are available Monday through Friday, 9 a.m. to 5 p.m. eastern time.

Bureau of Justice Assistance Information

General Information

Callers may contact the U.S. Department of Justice Response Center for general information or specific needs, such as assistance in submitting grant applications and information on training. To contact the Response Center, call 1–800–421–6770 or write to 1100 Vermont Avenue NW., Washington, DC 20005.

Indepth Information

For more indepth information about BJA, its programs, and its funding opportunities, requesters can call the BJA Clearinghouse. The BJA Clearinghouse, a component of the National Criminal Justice Reference Service (NCJRS), shares BJA program information with state and local agencies and community groups across the country. Information specialists are available to provide reference and referral services, publication distribution, participation and support for conferences, and other networking and outreach activities. The Clearinghouse can be reached by

❏ Mail
P.O. Box 6000
Rockville, MD 20849–6000

❏ Visit
2277 Research Boulevard
Rockville, MD 20850

❏ Telephone
1–800–688–4252
Monday through Friday
8:30 a.m. to 7 p.m.
eastern time

❏ Fax
301–519–5212

❏ Fax on Demand
1–800–688–4252

❏ BJA Home Page
www.ojp.usdoj.gov/BJA

❏ NCJRS World Wide Web
www.ncjrs.org

❏ E-mail
askncjrs@ncjrs.org

❏ JUSTINFO Newsletter
E-mail to listproc@ncjrs.org
Leave the subject line blank
In the body of the message, type:
subscribe justinfo
[your name]

www.ingramcontent.com/pod-product-compliance
Lightning Source LLC
Chambersburg PA
CBHW061517180526
45171CB00001B/212